W9-BUZ-383

...AND THERE WAS LIGHT

Books in print by Rocco A. Errico

Setting A Trap for God: The Aramaic Prayer of Jesus
Let There Be Light: The Seven Keys
And There Was Light
The Mysteries of Creation: The Genesis Story
*The Message of Matthew: An Annotated Parallel Aramaic-English Gospel
of Matthew*
Classical Aramaic – Book 1

Spanish publication
La Antigua Oración Aramea de Jesus: El Padrenuestro

German publications
Acht Einstimmungen auf Gott: Vaterunser
Es Werde Licht

Italian publication
Otto accordi con Dio: il Padre Nostro originario

Books in print by Rocco A. Errico and George M. Lamsa
Aramaic New Testament Series: Volumes 1 – 5
Aramaic Light on the Gospel of Matthew
Aramaic Light on the Gospels of Mark and Luke
Aramaic Light on the Gospel of John
Aramaic Light on the Acts of the Apostles
Aramaic Light on Romans – 2 Corinthians

...AND THERE WAS LIGHT

Rocco A. Errico

The Noohra Foundation, Inc
Smyrna, Georgia

Second Printing September 2004

ISBN: 0-9631292-5-2

In gratitude

to

Arllyn and Donalyn Kling

CONTENTS

PART ONE
Commentaries on the
Ministry and Teachings of Jesus

PART TWO
Commentaries
Here and There in Scripture

A Word from the Author

Treasures from the Language of Jesus made its first appearance in September 1987. This book adhered to the same style and tradition of my first published volume *Let There Be Light: The Seven Keys*. In the book "Treasures" I continued using the seven keys that explained numerous scriptural passages from the Aramaic language and biblical Near Eastern viewpoint. I had promised in my former book that there would be a follow up volume to *Let There Be Light*. Now, in this book, *And There Was Light,* a total revision and expansion of the book *Treasures from the Language of Jesus*, I have added more than 175 pages of new information. I have also rewritten all former material, expanding and clarifying its subject matter.

The Purpose of the Book

The purpose of the book is to present an alternative route, a Near Eastern route, that one may take in searching and studying Scripture. I apply the seven keys to specific biblical passages that people have puzzled over and have inquired of me over the years. For example, many have written to me requesting further insight into the life and teachings of Jesus. Therefore, I have included a general picture of Rabbi Eshoa—Jesus, an Aramaic speaking Shemite, before commenting on his ministry and teachings. I do not venture into Jesus' early life. There is very little information available on this topic. However, Dr. George M. Lamsa's book *The Hidden Years of Jesus* is a short but excellent look into the early life of Jesus.

A Review of the Seven Keys

For those readers who are not familiar with the seven keys, they are:

1. The Semitic languages of Aramaic and Hebrew.
2. Idioms in the Bible.
3. Near Eastern Biblical Mysticism.
4. Ancient Semitic Culture (customs and manners).
5. Near Eastern Psychology.
6. Near Eastern Symbolism.
7. Near Eastern Amplification.[1]

As with my first publication *Let There Be Light: The Seven Keys*, I wrote this book based on my ten years of intensive education with Dr. George M. Lamsa, knowledge of Aramaic and Hebrew languages, and my continued research of biblical Near Eastern studies and findings. Although this book differs from critical source/historical and literary methods in contemporary academic analysis of the Bible, it does include some of their insights and conclusions. Additionally, the information also derives from my seminars and articles that I have written and presented for the past 25 years along with new data.

The intention of this book is to focus on Semitic, English translations of biblical Aramaic texts and on the Near Eastern Semitic culture. This will aid us in expanding our knowledge of Scripture. It is also my aim to communicate these scriptural lessons so that we may apply them in our lives. In the various

---

[1]For a detailed explanation of the Seven Keys, see Rocco A. Errico, *Let There Be Light: The Seven Keys*, "Introduction" pp. xxv-xxxv, Noohra Foundation, 1994.

chapters, the reader will also find not just biblical history but metaphysical and practical interpretations to most of the scriptural texts.

The style of writing is a simple, direct approach using popular, everyday language without the use of critical or theological terminology.

The Format of the Book

The book is arranged in the following manner:

Preface: A brief introduction on the meaning of the term "Bible."

Part One: Commentaries on the ministry and teaching of Jesus (Baptism to Ascension).

Part Two: Commentaries—Here and there in Scripture (both Old and New Testaments).

Quotations

All scriptural quotes and references that read "Aramaic Peshitta text" are my English translations of the Aramaic texts of the Tanakh (O.T.) and the New Testament. When I cite the King James Version of the Bible, it is noted as "KJV." At times I also use the Lamsa English translation of the Aramaic Peshitta Bible. It is noted as the Lamsa translation. I have also referenced other citations from various authors in the footnotes. Let the reader understand that none of the chapters in this book is an exhaustive study on any particular topic. These chapters represent an overall view of the Bible through "Eastern eyes," applying the meanings of Semitic words, customs, and their spiritual and metaphysical principles and applications.

Acknowledgments and a Final Word

My sincere desire is that you enjoy this book and that you find the knowledge not only enlightening but helpful and nourishing to your heart and spirit. My deep heartfelt thanks to Ms. Sue Edwards, Ms. Ann Milbourn, and Ms. Linetta Izenman for their constructive suggestions and assistance with this manuscript. And to all my readers, I say to you: *"taybootha wshlama nehwoon amhon hasha walmeen."* Grace (loving-kindness) and peace are with you now and always!

August 1998

ABBREVIATIONS

Old Testament		New Testament	
Gen.	Genesis	Mt.	Matthew
Ex.	Exodus	Mk.	Mark
Lev.	Leviticus	Lk.	Luke
Dt.	Deuteronomy	Jn.	John
1 Sam.	1 Samuel	1 Cor.	1 Corinthians
1 Chron.	2 Chronicles	2 Cor.	2 Corinthians
Ps.	Psalms	Eph.	Ephesians
Isa.	Isaiah	2 Tim.	2 Timothy
Mic.	Micah	Heb.	Hebrews
Zeph.	Zephaniah	1 Jn.	1 John
Zech.	Zechariah	3 Jn.	3 John
Mal.	Malachi	Rev.	Revelation

Other Abbreviations

BCE	Before the common era, BC
CE	Common Era, AD
KJV	King James Version

Preface

The Term Bible

Our English term "Bible" comes from the Old French *bible*. The French word derives from the Latin and Greek *biblia* which means "books" or a "library of books." In English, we are accustomed to calling the Hebrew and Christian scriptures "Holy Bible." However, in ancient times, people did not ordinarily refer to this holy book as "Holy Bible." According to the Jewish writers Philo and Josephus, the usual term was the "Writings" or "Scriptures."

Its Semitic Meaning

In the Semitic languages of Aramaic and Hebrew, the term "Bible" is not used at all. In Hebrew, the name of the Holy Bible is *torah*. Although most scholars translate this Semitic word *torah* as the "law," it has a much deeper meaning. Originally *torah* referred to the first five books of Moses, Genesis through Deuteronomy. Later in history, Jewish people also used *torah* to refer to the entire Hebrew sacred writings. (See p. xxi, Tanakh.)

The Aramaic speaking Semites called the sacred writing *auretha* (pronounced *oraytha*). According to Aramaic and Hebrew lexicons both words, *torah* and *auretha,* derive from the Semitic root *yrh* and mean "to direct," "to teach," "to instruct," and by inference "to enlighten." Thus, the book we call "Holy Bible" is a book of directions, instructions, teachings, or enlightenment. Aramaic speakers preferred to render *torah* and

xix

auretha as "teaching" and "enlightenment."[1]

We cannot comprehend spiritual truths and principles through the human eye, nor can we easily explain these principles with words alone. We discern and understand spiritual ideas through the spiritual capacity of the mind. In other words, we realize genuine religious and spiritual truths by the faculty of our imagination. For example, it is Jesus' own religious genius and spiritual imagination that gave birth to his joyful message (gospel) of God's kingdom. He used stories to explain God's active presence in the world.

We need to understand the entire Bible from the Near Eastern and religious imagination of the ancient Semites. This book not only contains spiritual principles and enlightenment but also the culture, law, drama, history, poetry, science, philosophy, and psychology of the ancient Mesopotamian world.

Books of the Bible

The Protestant version of the Bible contains sixty-six books divided into two parts which Christians call Old and New Testaments. The New Testament with its twenty-seven so-called books is not a part of the *torah*. Jewish religious authorities do not refer to their holy Scripture as the Old Testament. They divide their sacred writings into three categories: *torah* — Law (Teaching or Enlightenment), *nevim* — Prophets, and *ketuvim* — Writings. From these three Hebrew words—*torah, nevim, and ketuvim*—Jewish scholars have created a modern acronym, *TNKH* (pronounced *Tanakh*) for their sacred book. *Tanakh*

---

[1]See Geza Vermes, *Jesus and the World of Judaism*, ch. 5, "Jewish Studies and New Testament Interpretation, p.71.

refers to the entire Hebrew Bible—Genesis through Malachi. The Catholic and Eastern Orthodox versions of the Bible contain seventy-three books.

A Divinely Authored Book

It is helpful to realize that the ancient Jewish sages did not consider that every single word or recorded episode in their holy book was divine revelation. These sages understood and believed that their "Torah was a divinely authored book, but they did not take the text literally. They took it seriously, but they always looked behind the flat, literal meaning."[2] We also need to understand that it is a book of recorded historical events[3] and Eastern tribal wars, along with their horrifying atrocities of violence. However, this does not necessarily mean clear cut history. (Interestingly, among Near Eastern, Assyrian Christians who lived in Northern Iraq, when the books of the law and

---

[2] W. Gunther Plaut, *The Torah—A Modern Commentary*, "Literalism." p. xvii.

[3] History writing in the Bible is different from today's style of historiography. Biblical authors often used literary devices for social and ideological purposes. See Marc Zvi Brettler, *The Creation of History in Ancient Israel*, Routledge, London and New York, 1995. "This study shows how the Hebrew Bible [Old Testament] can be used as a historical source. It strikes a balance between the position that the Bible is fictitious and the position that the Bible is completely true. The claims that the Hebrew Bible should be read as literature and as history are also explored." Brettler shows how the biblical historians were influenced by four key factors: typology, interpretation of earlier texts, satire, and ideology.

prophets were read aloud, they would stand. However, when all other portions of Scripture were read, these people would sit.)

We also need to understand that not all scripture is the Word of God. The hands of human beings penned this book. Some of it is revelation; other portions of scripture are not divine revelation. The Bible contains the Word of God as the prophets spoke it: "For prophecy at no time ever came by the will of human beings, but holy men of God spoke when they were impelled by the Holy Spirit."[4] Again it says: "All Scripture that is written by the inspiration of the Spirit is useful for teaching, correction, right action, and for instruction in piety."[5]

Conclusion

The Bible is a record of a nation's spiritual growth with its ups and downs. Metaphysically, it also tells the story of transcending consciousness. It records human encounters with the ineffable Presence we call God. And it is a book that tells the story of Israel's realization and understanding of God.

However, one of the most important facts we, as readers, must always keep in mind is that these recorded encounters, whether factual history or sacred stories, took place in the ancient Near East. Therefore, we must always consider the Semitic, Near Eastern culture and times when attempting to understand the Hebrew Bible and the New Testament.

---

[4] 2 Peter 1:21, Aramaic Peshitta text.

[5] 2 Tim. 3:16, Aramaic Peshitta text.

PART ONE

Commentaries on the
Ministry and Teachings of Jesus

Rabbi Eshoa—Jesus
An Aramaic Speaking Shemite[1]

Within our century there has been a dramatic and increasing number of volumes written on the life of Jesus and his teachings. As our century draws to a close, the last two decades have seen even more volumes written about Jesus than previously published. Despite all of our critical historical research and constructs, the man Jesus remains somewhat of a mystery. Undoubtedly, we will never fully and completely understand the man from Galilee.

However, we needlessly multiply our difficulties by taking Jesus out of his Near Eastern, Semitic environment. We constantly think of him in terms of modern Western Christianity. We see him through Church dogmas and creeds, through denominational beliefs, and through the context of our complex social world.

This presentation of Jesus is not a critical historical analysis of the Nazarene teacher-prophet. My intent is to bring the reader into the Eastern Mediterranean setting, the Aram-Mesopotamian culture and language. It is from this very culture that the dramatic and impelling life of the famous Galilean Jew appears to us. Hopefully, it will enhance the reader's perception of Jesus in his own Aramaic-Hebrew culture, religion, and social atmosphere.

---

[1]I originally wrote this essay for *The Book Your Church Doesn't Want You To Read*, Editor Tim Leedom, 1993. The essay as it appears here is a total revision.

Jesus' Native Background

Ethnically speaking, Jesus was a Shemite. In English we drop the letter "h" in Shemite. We spell and pronounce the word as "Semite." The term "Shemite" comes from one of the sons of Noah whose name was Shem.[2] This expression "Shemite" applies to many Semitic dialects. It also refers to all the descendants of Shem, such as the Akkadians, Arameans, Assyrians, Chaldeans, Hebrews and Arabs.

What kind of general temperament does a native-born Near Easterner, especially a Semite, possess? What of his manner of speech and his deep religious feelings? What would be his accustomed outlook on life? As we find the answers to these questions, we can see, at least in part, the human Jesus emerging from his own inherited Semitic, psychological element. We can have a clearer sense of the man Jesus and his teachings as we begin to appreciate the rich cultural and religious philosophy of his time in its multi-level Judaic context.

The Four Gospels

The gospels of Matthew, Mark, Luke, and John are the main sources to help us uncover the Semitic Jesus. Modernly speaking, these gospel writings are not biographical material about Jesus. The truth is that no contemporary stylized biographies exist anywhere in holy Scripture from Genesis to the last book of the New Testament. As a general rule, ancient Near Easterners had no deep interest in the details of a great man's life from birth to death. Their basic interest in such a man would be in his

---

[2]See Gen. 5:32.

teachings and the overall impact of those teachings upon their lives.

The authors of the four gospels wrote their material quite sometime after Jesus' death. These writings began as recollections of his words and acts as a teacher—an honored rabbi, prophet, and healer. Early Church scribes added the birth, death, and resurrection stories to the acts and teachings of Jesus much later.

However, we must not think that the gospel texts are mythical creations just because the historians of Jesus' day did not mention him in their writings.[3] We need to realize that Jesus was a provincial rabbi[4] from a small village in Galilee. He was not widely known. Jesus' primary human characteristics were, probably, no different from the basic human traits of anyone else in his community. He distinguished himself because he rose above conventional wisdom of his day. An unusual and powerful teacher, Jesus presented a new and revolutionary understanding of Israel's God. Today most modern historians and scholars, in general, no longer doubt Jesus' historical existence.[5]

---

[3]There are a few, Flavius Josephus being one of them.

[4]The term "rabbi" was just emerging during the early part of the first century C.E. It was an honorific term showing great respect to an outstanding teacher. Literally "rabbi" means "my great one." The technical use of "rabbi" as we now know and understand it did not fully develop until the end of the 2nd century C.E.

[5]See John P. Meir, *A Marginal Jew: Rethinking the Historical Jesus*, "Sources: Josephus, Other Pagan and Jewish Writings, The Agrapha and the Apocryphal Gospels" pp. 56-184.

How Reliable Are the Gospels?

For the last two and a half centuries, the four gospels have been and continue to be the subject of many scholarly and not so scholarly historical debates, academic research, and fiery discussion. Despite the disagreement among scholars and the fact that the writers and editors of the gospels present us with a partial and theologically colored portrait of Jesus, we can still find the human, Semitic, Nazarene teacher within their pages. We must consider and include this vital point in the search for the human Jesus.

For example, the late Lebanese scholar, Dr. Abraham M. Rihbany,[6] tells us that he read the gospels not as documents that he had to scrutinize "to establish the historicity of concrete reports." He says that "they read like letters written from his hometown in Lebanon." Of course, Dr. Rihbany was much in favor of historical research, but his emphasis was on the inherent nature of Semitic people—an aspect which many scholars often overlook. In his book *The Syrian Christ,* he gives his penetrating point of view very clearly and succinctly:

> In the Gospel story of Jesus' life there is not a single incident that is not in perfect harmony with the prevailing modes of thought and the current speech of the land of its origin. It is most natural, that the Gospel truths should have come down to the succeeding generation—and to the nations of the West—cast in Oriental [Near Eastern] molds of thought, and intimately intermingled with the simple domestic and social habits of Syria [Aram]. The gold of the Gospel carries with it the sand and dust of its original home.

---

[6]Dr. Rihbany, a Semite, was a dedicated minister and an adept, prolific writer/author on Near Eastern customs and manners.

I was born not far from where the Master was born, and brought up under almost the identical conditions under which he lived. I have an inside view of the Bible which by the nature of things, a Westerner cannot have. And I know that the conditions of life in Syria of today are essentially as they were in the time of Christ, not from the study of the mutilated tablets of the archaeologist and the antiquarian....but from the simple fact that, as a sojourner in this Western world, whenever I open my Bible it reads like a letter from home. Its unrestrained effusiveness of expression; its vivid, almost flashy and fantastic imagery; its naive narrations; the rugged unstudied simplicity of its parables; its unconventional portrayal of certain human relations; as well as its all permeating spiritual mysticism . . .might all have been written in my primitive village home, on the western slope of Mount Lebanon some thirty years ago. . .

The need of Western readers of the Bible is, in my judgment, to enter sympathetically and intelligently into the atmosphere in which the books of the Scriptures first took form; to have real intellectual, as well as spiritual fellowship, with those Orientals [Near Easterners] who sought earnestly in their own way to give tangible form to those great spiritual truths which have been, and ever shall be, humanity's most precious heritage.[7]

Jesus' Own Language, People and Times

Let us view Rabbi Jesus, an Aramaic speaking Shemite, in the light of his own language, people, and times. We are going

---

[7]Abraham M. Rihbany, *The Syrian Christ*, pp. vi-vii, 4-6, and 12, published 1916.

to examine the background of the ancient Aramaic language,[8] Hebrew Scripture, customs, metaphors, and psychology, as well as the unencumbered Aramaic style of writing behind the teachings and narratives of the gospels.

According to Matthew and Luke, Jesus was born of unassuming parents in a rural, modest town in the province of Galilee.[9] He grew up among humble people to whom simplicity and poverty were the highest realities in life. These country peasants did not speak or think in sophisticated ways. Jesus proclaimed and taught his message with simple words coming from daily speech and illustrated with stories that everyone could understand.

However, in a broader setting, Jesus came into a world that the great Roman empire was ruling. Rome had established peace and order. Its military organization and institutions were unequaled by any other nation until the beginning of the 20th century. Rome's laws were universal.

To this day the Galilean teacher receives ongoing world-wide acclaim and worship through many forms, yet he never sought worshipers. He never attempted to inaugurate a new system of worship. Nor did he wish to undermine the genuine underpinnings of his forefather's religion. He discounted honors and notoriety. He came not for humankind to sacrifice to him, but that he might serve humanity.

From a historical perspective, it is certain that Jesus never thought of himself as possessing any superhuman nature. Nor was he conscious of any unusual, supernatural birth. Church scribes created these ideas and added them to the gospels when they were compiled. His immediate disciples who were also

---

[8]See appendix on: *A Brief History of the Aramaic Language.*

[9]Most likely Nazareth.

from Galilee knew him as the son of Mary and Joseph. Jesus was a citizen of Nazareth. And this is exactly the way in which Simon Peter declared Jesus on the Jewish feast day of Pentecost. "Men and sons of Israel, hear these words: ***Jesus of Nazareth, a man of God***, who appeared among you. . . ." [10]

The gospels themselves testify to Jesus' limitations as a human being. Anthony C. Deane, Canon of Windsor, says: "St. Mark is not afraid to attribute human limitations to our Lord; he feels grief, anger, surprise, amazement, fatigue; he asks questions for information; at times he is unable to do what he wills."[11] Though the humanity of Jesus appears in the gospels, the theology that developed in and among the early communities of believers (around the latter half of the first century C.E.) began to overlay Jesus' historical sayings and to obscure his essential human nature.

Jesus the Human Being

As Jesus grew and matured, his interaction with his environment and his clear comprehension of the needs of his people made him conscious of his destiny. He thought of himself as a "son of God" in the Judaic context of his time. He never claimed that he was God's only son! Jesus felt himself to be fully human. Deep faith and his personal relationship with God whom he called "Father" motivated him. He taught no abstruse and mysterious doctrines. He did not wait for people to come to him. Jesus went to the people.

When he taught, he did so in the synagogues, marketplaces,

---

[10] Acts 2:22, Aramaic Peshitta text.

[11] Anthony C. Deane, How to Understand the Gospels, p. 48.

7

at private homes, on hilltops, at the seashore, and anywhere else he could find listeners. The Galilean master originated no difficult terms to understand; he used familiar ideas. His comforting, charismatic personality and his plain words and direct parables captivated the harried Galileans who eagerly sought him and listened to him.

He called God *Abba*, "Father." He ascribed to God, by implication, a universal and special providence, humane in its action, doing good even to the ungrateful and the wicked. He also ascribed to his Father a benevolent ethical nature. According to Jesus, God's nature consisted of gracious love, a spirit delighting in compassion and ready to forgive, and desiring that same spirit to rule in everyone's heart and soul. Jesus, in eloquent simplicity, taught from a deep assurance that a human being, regardless of imperfections, carries within his or her soul the transcendent power of God.

The Near Eastern Temperament

The best way to understand Near Eastern temperament and daily language of Semites is to receive first-hand information from a Near Easterner. Dr. Abraham M. Rihbany tells us the following:

> The Oriental [Near Easterner] I have in mind is the Semite, the dweller of the Near East, who, chiefly through the Bible, has exerted an immense influence on the life and literature of the West. The son of the Near East is more emotional, more intense, and more communicative than his Far-Eastern neighbors. Although very old in point of time, his (the Semite) temperament remains somewhat juvenile and his manner of speech intimate and unreserved. From

the remote past, even to this day, the Oriental's [Near Easterner's] manner of speech has been that of a worshiper, and not that of a business man or an industrial worker in the modern Western sense. . . .His daily language is essentially biblical. He has no secular language. The only real break between his Scriptures and the vocabulary of his daily life is that which exists between the classical and the vernacular. . . .

An Easterner's chief purpose in a conversation is to convey an impression by whatever suitable means, and not to deliver his message in scientifically accurate terms. He piles up his metaphors and superlatives, reinforced by a theatrical display of gestures and facial expression in order to make the hearer feel his meaning. He speaks as it were in pictures. With him the spoken language goes hand in hand with the most ancient gesture language. His profuse gesticulation is the phase of his life which first challenges the attention of Western travelers in the East. He points to almost everything he mentions in his speech and would portray every feeling and emotion by means of some bodily movement. . . .

It is also because he loves to speak in pictures and to subordinate literal accuracy to the total impression of an utterance, that he makes such extensive use of figurative language. Instead of saying to the Pharisees, *Your pretensions to virtue and good birth far exceed your actual practice of virtue*, John the Baptist cried: *Oh generation of vipers, etc.* Just as he loves to flavor his food strongly and to dress in bright colors, so is he fond of metaphor, exaggeration, and positiveness in speech. To him mild accuracy is weakness.

The supreme choice of the Oriental [Near Easterner] has been religion. To say that this choice has not been altogether a conscious one, that it has been the outcome of temperament, does by no means lessen its significance.

9

From the beginning of his history on the earth to this day the Oriental [Semite] has been conscious above all things of two supreme realities—**God and the soul**. What has always seemed to him to be his first and almost only duty was and is to form the most direct, most intimate connection between God and the soul. The **fear of the Lord**, meaning **most affectionate reverence**, is to the son of the East not the beginning of wisdom as the English Bible has it, but the height or acme of wisdom. His first concern about his children is that they should know themselves as living souls and God as their Creator and Father.[12]

It is from this Near Eastern psychological background, religious temperament and language that not only the gospels' portraits of Jesus come to us, but also the Bible in its entirety. Jesus' genetic nature was that of a Shemite. He was, without a doubt, dramatic and demonstrative in speech and action, able to make an indelible impression on his followers and listeners.

In the chapters and commentaries that follow this brief profile on Jesus of Nazareth, I depict aspects of his life in his Semitic, Aramaic setting. I emphasize the purely human side of Jesus as we find it in the gospels.

In his own incarnation, he was a Shemite—a son of the Near East. But in his spiritual and religious nature, Jesus of Nazareth was unique. He belongs to the entire human family in every generation and in every age. Many of the Aramaic terms attributed to Jesus, or those that he may have used himself (some of which no longer carry the original meaning), have been misunderstood over the centuries—such terms as "Son of God," "Son of Man," "Messiah-Christ," and many other titles bestowed on him.

---

[12]Rihbany, *The Syrian Christ*, pp. 81, 84, 115-116.

The Apostle Paul and Jesus

Before concluding, one other point needs mentioning. Paul, a visionary who had the ability to enter altered states of consciousness (trance states), cast Jesus in yet another role. To Paul, Jesus was a mystical Messiah—a mystical Christ—the heavenly man who conquered principalities and powers of the air. He added his messianic revelation to the already prevailing ideas which were adopted and attributed to Jesus by the second generation of believers.

There is no evidence that the members of the Jerusalem Church accepted Paul's interpretation of Jesus as the mystical Christ. On the contrary, because of Paul's liberalism, the Church at first refused to extend to Paul the hand of fellowship. The leaders of the Jerusalem Church finally made a compromise with him that he would preach to the Gentiles and they to the Jews.

It was easy for the Greeks, who at that time led the world in philosophy, to accept Paul's ideas of a mystical Christ. Jesus' immediate disciples who walked, talked, and sailed with him on the lake of Galilee never for a moment thought they were associating with the Creator of heaven and earth. The bond of union among the Jewish believers in Jesus was more fraternal than creedal. What they had in common was their devotion to their teacher and his teachings.

Conclusion

Jesus, a Shemite, a man among men, and a teacher of teachers, continues to speak throughout all the ages. His human personality, his loving nature, and his simple teachings will live forever. They will always continue to enrich and embrace the hearts of the human family everywhere.

When we come to fully realize the unpretentious teachings of Jesus, all subtle forms of imperialism that advocate absolutism—such as an infallible Church, infallible Bible, infallible doctrines, or infallible anything—will no longer stand. Our human desire for infallibility is a lust for undisputed authority and absolute power. It seeks to dominate individual freedom and free thought.

Violence, hatred, and prejudice have no place in the presence of compassion, truth and harmony which is God's kingdom. Jesus taught God's sovereignty working in and through our ordinary, mundane living. The human Jesus was a simple man. His source was God. His spiritual insight continues to ignite the hearts and souls of men, women, and children the world over.

1

In My Name

Never, in all world history, is there a name that has received such universal acclaim as that of the Jewish prophet and teacher, Jesus of Nazareth. Almost two thousand years have elapsed since his crucifixion, death and resurrection. Yet, his name is just as meaningful today as the day the angel Gabriel announced it to Mary (Miriam) in a vision.

Many people all over the world invoke the name of "Jesus" in their private devotions, in public prayers and ceremonies, in healing services, and in times of great distress and need. There are also a great many religious debates and controversies that surround this popular name. Jesus' name has been equated with God, love, power, meekness, suffering, compassion, and understanding. This name has also been connected with religious wars, prejudice, hatred, and acts of violence. These facts are well known. But what does it mean when John's gospel advises us "to pray and believe in his name?"

The Meaning of Jesus Name

Our English rendering of the name "Jesus" comes directly from the Greek language—*Iesous*. This is the Greek equivalent of the Hebrew *Yehoshua*—Joshua in English. In Aramaic, the Northern Galilean form of the name is *Yeshoa* or *Eshoa*.

This name was a common and popular one in biblical lands during and before the first century. Its meaning from the Hebrew and Aramaic languages is "Yahweh saves or helps."[1] We need to ask: Does this name contain some sort of mystical power? Could simply intoning the name "Jesus" make spiritual forces and divine wonders active in one's life? Or is there something else to understand when we utter this name? What is the idea behind praying "in Jesus' name?" Is there a method that we can learn so as to effectively apply this name to meet present, everyday problems?

Let us examine Jesus' words from his own native tongue, Aramaic, to answer these questions. We need to return to Jesus' time and to the pure Semitic idea and thought behind the use of his name. According to the writer of the gospel of John, Jesus told his disciples that they would be doing certain things "in his name." Jesus' apostles, in turn, admonished others to "believe in his name."

Matthew's gospel reports Jesus saying: "For wherever two or three are gathered together *in my name*, I am there among them."[2] Mark, in his gospel, also reports that Jesus instructed his disciples to go into all the world and preach his gospel to the whole creation and "Wonders will follow those who believe these things. *In my name* they will cast out demons (Aramaic: heal the mentally ill). They will speak with new tongues. They will handle snakes (Aramaic: they will be able to handle those who oppose his teaching). And if they should drink any poison of death, it will not harm them (Aramaic: they will overcome vicious gossip and attacks against their character). And they will lay hands on the sick and they will be healed."[3]

---

[1]For a detailed account of the name "Jesus," Rocco A. Errico, *Let There Be Light: The Seven keys*, "The Name of Jesus," pp. 184-186.

[2]Mt. 18:20, Aramaic Peshitta text.

[3]Mk. 16:17-18, Aramaic Peshitta text.

The power to do all these things such as healing the mentally ill, handling the opposition without harm, speak in a new language, creating wonders, would be "in his name." Again, Jesus said: "What I say to you is absolutely true that anything you may ask my Father *in my name*, he will give it to you. Until now you have asked nothing *in my name*. Ask and you will receive so that your joy may be full."[4]

The Aramaic Meaning

Beshemi, in Aramaic, means "in my name," and it infers "in my way, method, or system of doing things." Another way to put it would be to do wonders, healing, and speaking "in or with my understanding or consciousness of life and God." More simply put: "Do it the way I have been doing it." To help us understand the idea, let me illustrate it with the work of Dr. Albert Einstein.

Physicists use Dr. Einstein's system or formula in splitting the atom. However, these scientists do not speak directly to the atom and say: "In the name of Einstein, atom split!" They use his method for splitting the atom. In a certain sense, every time these scientific doctors split the atom, they do so in Einstein's name. But they do not utter his name while going through the scientific procedure.

Yet many ardent believers use Jesus' name in this very manner and expect something magical to take place by uttering the name "Jesus." Sometimes things do occur for those sincere people. This is because their faith, love, and devotion to Jesus of Nazareth expresses itself while uttering his name. However,

---

[4]Jn. 16:23-24, Aramaic Peshitta text.

15

other seekers of truth have prayed applying "Jesus' name" and have wondered why nothing happened at all.

Merely uttering the name "Jesus" will not bring about the desired results any more than just pronouncing the name of Einstein would cause the atom to split. What brings about the outcome is practicing and understanding Jesus' way of doing things. One must learn his method or "formula."

Jesus' Method

We need to work with and implement Jesus' teaching. He had spiritual equations that set men, women, and children free from all kinds of physical, mental, and emotional bonds. The so-called secret of "Jesus' name," then, is to realize, to experience, and to understand the same spiritual equations or mental equivalents as Jesus.

His "formula" is very simple. But we must participate in it and make it a part of our consciousness and way of living. Our hearts, minds, spirits and souls must become one with the idea. Our faith, love, and emotions must connect with a consciousness that knows:

That God who is life, health, and goodness itself is a loving presence.

That this loving presence is everyone's source of all good and all joy.

That every individual is fully capable of demonstrating the good she or he truly expects and anticipates from that very source we call God.

That we are not helpless creatures—we are children of the living God.

That God who is life and joy is all that we need.

That our faith, love, and devotion are one with this living presence and source of all life.

Jesus' Name Is the Way

Jesus' approach to God and people was totally refreshing. He was not like other religious teachers of his day, who were concerned with outward forms of religion. He did not bother with man-made doctrines, hairsplitting dogmas, and ritualism.

Jesus took a comparatively small group of simple young men from Galilee and taught them the principles of God's kingdom (sovereignty). Through these illiterate young men, he changed the course of history. Their master demonstrated to them what it really meant to be a "child of God." He endowed these simple men with spiritual insight and gifts to aid all humanity. Jesus' idea of a universal, loving Intelligence (Presence), whom he called "Father," transformed his followers.

These followers, through their Master's teaching, transcended their old living styles. When the total realization of Jesus' way dawns upon us, we too will understand the transcending power that there is "in Jesus' name."

2

The Messiah—Christ

"Messiah" is the anglicized form of the Aramaic and Hebrew terms *m'shiha* and *mashiach*. In Aramaic it is pronounced as *m'sheeha*. Both the Aramaic and the Hebrew terms come from the Semitic root *m'shakh*. The verbal form means "to smear," "to anoint," "to oil," "to rub over," " to ordain," "to consecrate," and literally, "to wipe or stroke with the hand."

When biblical translators rendered this Semitic word from both of the Near Eastern tongues of Aramaic and Hebrew into the Western language of Greek, the term *Christos* came into existence. As we can easily see, our English word "Christ" derives from the Greek language. Translators merely dropped the letters "os" that appear in the Greek word *Christos*.

The Semitic noun *m'shiha* or *mashiach* means "Anointed One," "Ordained One," and by inference, "Appointed One." This noun also means "oil," "ointment," or a "consecrated person or thing." Thus, Messiah-Christ is one who is ordained, anointed, and appointed. The term "Christ" also connotes one who carries the light of God. (Near Easterners also used oil as fuel for their light.) A Christ is one who embodies light and truth.

Messiah-Christ on an esoteric level refers to an anointed heart and soul that are filled with love and understanding. An enlightened mind is a "Christed" individual. Thus, the term "Christ" not only designates Jesus of Nazareth, but it also points to all those who realize and actualize their own divine sonship through the Christ. "But to those who accepted him [Christ], he gave them the authority (right) to become children of God, to

18

those who believe in his name."[1]

The Anointed Priesthood

In the Tanakh (Old Testament), biblical authors used this term to designate "anointed one" or "ordained one." Moses had ordained Aaron as high priest and his sons as priests with oil. Therefore, they were "consecrated ones." Through this anointing they were ordained and dedicated to the service of God. (See Exodus 28:41.) The high priest, in particular, was the "Christ (Anointed) of God." (See Leviticus 4:3, 5, 16.)

Anointed Kings and Prophets

When Israel established a monarchy, the same Semitic term *mashiach* expressed the idea of an "anointed" king. He was the "anointed (Christ) of the Lord." The king received the anointing oil upon his head in a ceremony that depicted the sacredness and responsibility of ruling God's people. He was consecrated into this high office, not sworn into office as king. Israel's kings needed to be aware of their responsibility to God. They had to carry out the care and protection of Yahweh's people and obey the divine laws given to Moses for themselves and for the nation. (See 1 Samuel 2:10, 35; 9:16; and 24:6.)

Another divinely appointed person was a prophet. (See 1 Kings 19:16.) Biblically speaking, there were three kinds of individuals who received the anointing—priests, kings and sometimes prophets. All these people, especially priest and king,

---

[1]Jn. 1:12, Aramaic Peshitta text.

were "Christs" in the sense of "ordained" and "anointed." The term "messiah" as we now understand it cannot be applied here. New Testament writers applied these three offices to Jesus of Nazareth as the Christ. He was King, Priest, and Prophet.

Jesus of Nazareth fulfilled the role as an appointed and ordained man. No one had literally anointed him. He had no organization behind him. God had appointed him for a tremendous task. He lived the role of "Messiah-Christ" from a perspective all his own and not from the usual interpretation of a messiah.

Jesus knew that world peace could come only by awakening latent spiritual forces that are inherent in humanity. Any form of government that embodies truth must be built on universal principles of justice, compassion, and understanding for all. Violence has no place in this form of government.

Jesus, as king, did not and does not need any earthly throne from which to rule. It was not necessary for him to raise an army and lead a revolution. His revolution was an inner one. The magnificent kingdom and throne he established were to be set in people's hearts and souls from all nations and races. In this sense, he truly is the Messiah-Christ.[2]

Although scholarly studies in the idea of the Messiah expectation in the first century is in a state of flux, we can see a partial picture of the times. Undoubtedly, in the hearts and minds of Israel at this time, there burned a strong desire and dream for a peaceful and joyful future. Prior to the reign of King David, the Hebrews had no thought of a Messiah.

The pre-exilic prophets had hoped and worked for their nation to cleanse itself morally so that Israel could become a

---

[2]For a detailed study on the term Messiah, I highly recommend: *The Messiah: Developments in Earliest Judaism and Christianity*, James H. Charlesworth, editor, Augsburg Fortress Press, 1992.

great beacon to guide all nations into paths of justice. According to Isaiah's vision, Israel, having cleansed itself, would then come under the leadership of a king from the family of David. Under the wise and powerful leadership of this predicted king, justice, peace, compassion, and national contentment would reign and abound throughout their land. There would be such a powerful change in state and secular affairs that other nations would also benefit from this national spiritual revival.

However, after the exile and return of the people of Judah to their homeland, known as the Second-Temple Era, the ideas of a future king began to change. From 167 B.C.E. to the time of the birth of Jesus, various messianic ideas were born and underwent many modifications. Malachi had predicted that Elijah would appear and prepare the way for the Lord. A human, earthly leader would have the necessary power to lead and fight for Israel.

More and more writings and predictions began to appear. Some said that the Messiah would be an aggressive, militant, and political leader who would destroy the enemies of God's people. Other groups anticipated the appearance of a supernatural Messiah. Many false messiahs began to make their appearances. These pretenders led the people into violent attacks against the Romans. But the iron hand of Rome quickly crushed them and their followers.

Almost all ancient religions expressed some sort of belief in a Savior. This was especially true whenever nations fell prey to hatred, injustice, persecution, and the devastation of war. People's hearts were filled with the hope that a power in the form of some great leader would bring national peace and salvation.

Zoroaster, the Prophet

In Persia (Iran) this idea came from the god Ormazd whose throne was in the endless light of heaven. Ormazd himself was light, life, and the soul of all that was pure and good. According to the legend, this Persian deity saw how humans were bent toward destruction. He understood that they were very weak. So he graciously determined to open the eyes of humanity by sending a prophet, Zoroaster, on a sacred mission. Zoroaster, like Jesus, believed that the kingdom of heaven was at hand and, along with his disciples, hoped to live long enough to witness its inauguration.

The Babylonian Prophecy

There exists a parallel Babylonian legend that is even more striking than the Persian legend. It predicted that wars and other tragedies must occur before the coming of a conquering Messiah or Leader. "Seacoast will rise against seacoast, Elamite against Elamite, Cassite against Cassite, country against country, house against house, man against man. Brother is to show no mercy toward a brother. They will kill one another."

This particular prediction was to continue until a certain time when the special Akkadian would come, overthrow and conquer them all. The prophecy concerned the arrival of the great King Hammurabi who was to initiate a golden age of peace in the fullness of time. Compare the above predictions with Mark 13:7-13. Keeping Mark's verses in mind we can see the many influences that Babylon (Chaldea) had exerted on the Jewish nation. Notice the striking resemblance between these two predictions.

During the first century C.E., many ideas concerning the Messiah were circulating throughout the land: a Prince-Messiah of the House of David, a Priest-King, a Warrior, a Mediator between God and man, a pre-existent Messiah, and a superhuman Messiah who would destroy Satan and his kingdom. (However, a word of caution—scholars are making deeper studies into the first century in Palestine and this picture may change somewhat.)

Nonetheless, Jesus, a provincial rabbi from half-heathen Galilee, with a small discipleship of fisherman and crowds of poor peasants who followed him, could not measure up to such expectations. Jesus could not meet the requirements set down for a great hero—"a Prince-Messiah of the House of David." We can now understand why Jesus forbade his immediate disciples to call him "Messiah." Jesus knew change could only come about when the human heart, mind, and soul would change and not just through one individual. The majority of humanity must participate in truth—not truth as a doctrine but as justice, peace, love, and understanding for all humankind!

3

The Baptism of Jesus

Matthew's gospel reports an event in the life of Jesus that has been an embarrassment to the Christian Church ever since this experience was first recorded:

> At that time Jesus came from Galilee to the Jordan to John so that he might be baptized by him. But John stopped him saying, I need to be baptized by you, and yet you come to me? Now Jesus answered and said to him, Let it be so for now, because it is necessary for us so that all goodness may be fulfilled. So he allowed him. Then when Jesus was baptized, and as soon as he came up out of the water, heaven was opened to him, and he saw the Spirit of God descending like a dove, and it settled on him.[1]

An Authentic Event

Scholars have debated the authenticity of this particular episode which began Jesus' ministry. Did John really baptize Jesus?[2] Most scholars, but not all, accept Jesus' baptism as authentic. The purpose of this writing is not a historical/critical

---

[1]Mt. 3:13-16, Aramaic Peshitta text.

[2]For a full treatment and discussion see John P. Meir, *A Marginal Jew: Rethinking the Historical Jesus,* "The Historicity of Jesus' Baptism by John" pp. 100-106, and "Jesus a Disciple of John?" pp. 116-130.

analysis of the episode. My approach is to understand Jesus' baptism from Near Eastern, Semitic customs and its meaning for us today. Let us now examine the story.

New Testament critics look upon John's refusal to baptize Jesus as a later Christian addition in the gospel narrative. However, if we follow the story as told in the synoptic gospels, John the Baptist and Jesus were cousins. The text implies that John knew that Jesus was greater than he. This is the reason he did not want to baptize Jesus.

John was also mindful of Eastern formality. Custom of the time dictated that people of high social standing often humbled themselves as a sign of social grace. For example, at a banquet a nobleman will say to one of a lower social status: "Please sit higher than I." Nonetheless, the man of lower social rank will insist that the nobleman occupy the higher seat. This is done to honor one another.

Although Jesus understood what John was doing, he did not pay any attention to Eastern formality. Jesus knew what his mission was about. He was identifying himself with his people. It was an act of solidarity with the people of Israel.

By submitting to the Baptist's water baptism, Jesus accepted John's message and acknowledged John's mission. The reported reply of Jesus to John was: "Let it be so for now, because it is necessary for us, so that all goodness may be fulfilled." As I said earlier, despite the fact that much later Christian scribes added to the narrative of Jesus' baptism, Jesus' response carries a simple but profound meaning for the hearers of the gospel story.

The Meaning of Righteousness

The King James version translates Jesus' reply as: "And

Jesus answered and said unto him, Suffer it to be so now: for thus it becometh us to fulfill all righteousness." What does the word "righteousness" mean in this verse? I translate it as "goodness." In Aramaic, *kenutha* means an authentic "piety," that is, "integrity." It also means "justice," "devoutness," "righteousness," "godliness," and "goodness." It refers, as well, to an ethical justice based on the Torah. Jesus did whatever was necessary for a just life, one full of integrity, because he was one with the Father.

Jesus showed his humility and meekness by identifying with his people and with John's message. He was concerned only with matters that were beneficial to humankind. Thus, at the River Jordan, Jesus humbled himself and let John baptize him. He revealed the true qualities of God. Through meekness and gentleness Jesus evinced a genuine spiritual leadership.

We need to realize that whatever Jesus manifested in his own life is also our potential as well. According to Hebrew Scripture, humanity is God's image and likeness.[3] Therefore, all humankind is also capable of manifesting God's qualities.

The Open Skies

"Heaven opened to him" is a Near Eastern expression that symbolizes a communication between heaven and earth. In other words, what was once a mystery or secret was now revealed. Through this Galilean sage and teacher, heavenly truth was to be revealed and realized in a new way. "Open skies" is another way of saying that the universe rejoiced because this man's presence would remove the chasm between heaven and earth. (This

---

[3]See Gen. 1:26-27.

chasm exists only in one's mind.)

The dove signifies meekness and purity, as well as peace, harmony, and tranquility. In the Near East, when describing a humble and gentle individual, people often say: "He is so good and harmless that even a dove will come and sit upon him," or "He is so meek that a bird will not fly away from him."

Spirit has neither shape nor form, but the Semitic writers of Scripture symbolized the Spirit as a dove so that common folk might grasp its meaning. Spirit as a dove settling on Jesus meant that Jesus was approved by God and that a new world order of peace and understanding was to replace the old order. Jesus was now ready to embark on his glorious mission. This would change the world and bring humanity to a greater understanding of God, and hence, to a greater understanding of itself and the meaning of life.

4

The Expectation

"After John had been delivered into the hands of King Herod, Jesus came to Galilee and he was announcing the joyful message of God's sovereign rule. And he was saying: The time is right, God's sovereign counsel has arrived! Turn to God and have confidence in this joyful hope."[1] According to Mark, Jesus entered Galilee declaring and demonstrating the power of God's presence among the people. Jesus' message of the kingdom of God was, beyond any doubt, the heart and core of all that he taught and practiced.

The Meaning of Kingdom and Gospel

The Aramaic the word for "gospel" is *swartha*. It also means "news that makes glad," "joyful hope, expectation." The gospel, then, is the joyful expectation or message. But, what joyful hope or message? People were anticipating God's sovereign rule. They were expecting God to act on their behalf. "Kingdom" in Aramaic is *malkutha*. Its root is *mlkh,* "to counsel, advise." Thus, the kingdom of God is actually God's sovereign counsel or reigning presence. Jesus used this expression "the kingdom of God" as a symbol that pointed to God's active presence in and among the people.

---

[1]Mk. 1:14-15, Aramaic Peshitta text.

The Reign of God

Israel was eagerly awaiting the coming of God's reign. From the time of the prophets to the days of Jesus, people held this long-cherished expectation in their hearts and minds. When Jesus made his appearance, he declared that God's kingdom was present and that their expectation would now find gratification. Jesus healed the afflicted, the infirm, and the severely mentally ill. He revealed to the people the mysteries of this heavenly kingdom through his parables and sayings.

In spite of Jesus' teachings and demonstrations of healing, people were expecting a literal, powerful political kingdom. They did not realize that the kingdom was already present and that its power worked to heal sick bodies and transform hearts and minds. Jesus had told his disciples and the Pharisees that the kingdom does not come by observation but that it was among them. (See Luke 17:20)

This spiritual reign of God was and is that of a nonpolitical, nonpartisan, international kingdom of genuine justice, peace, and joy. Its rule would come from the hearts of its subjects in any time or age. God's kingdom would naturally infiltrate the political and social life of its adherents. This kingdom was a celebration of life and all people regardless of race or lifestyle. Jesus welcomed sinners, tax collectors, and prostitutes. He understood the nature of this kingdom and that only a kingdom that was established within the very hearts of its denizens could possibly last throughout the ages.

World peace will only manifest fully when the majority of its leaders and inhabitants discover the true peace of God's counsel within themselves. We must realize that force and violence will never bring the harmony we need. War is only a temporary fix. Legal force cannot hold back violence forever. We have seen people rebel and use force and violence to bring down dictatorships. The way in which we obtain something is the same way in which we have to maintain it. There is only one answer to our dilemma. We must turn to a presence that is greater than our human thoughts and ways. We must turn to what we call God.

Prophets, Jesus, and the apostles called the people to repentance. The Aramaic meaning of the word to "repent" is "to do an about face," "to turn completely around"—that is, "to turn to God." When we turn to God, we turn to the true essence of our beings. We turn to the powers of love, harmony, and understanding that are present within us. We are God's children, heirs of the kingdom.

5

Uncovering Jesus' Gospel

The term "gospel" can be confusing. For example, the New Testament opens with four gospels: *The Gospel according to St. Matthew, The Gospel according to St. Mark, The Gospel according to St. Luke*, and *The Gospel according to St. John*. New Testament scholars also refer to the apostle Paul's writing and teaching as: *The Gospel according to St. Paul*, although none of his works actually carry this title. Today, most of us know or hear about the *Evangelical Gospel* preached via radio or television.[1] But, do any or all these so-called "gospels" truly represent the *Gospel according to Jesus*?

Three Distinct Words

New Testament translators usually render three distinct Aramaic words—*swartha, evangalion, karozutha*—into English as "gospel." This is where the confusion begins with the meaning of the word "gospel" in English. Let's look into these three distinct words:

1. *Swartha* does translate as "gospel." It derives from the Aramaic root *swr*, meaning to "hope," "trust," "announce," "declare," "tell," "bring news," and "publish abroad." Thus, one may translate *swartha* as the joyful "message," " hope," or "expectation." An appropriate rendering into English would

---

[1]This phenomenon is known as "electronic evangelism."

depend on the scriptural context.

2. *Evangalion* comes directly from Greek, although some Aramaic language experts dispute this notion. They claim that *evangalion* originated from Aramaic. However, Aramaic nouns that terminate in "ion" are loan words from Greek. *Evangalion* has the same meaning as the Greek word *evangel*, "good news." Certain Aramaic linguists say that this word in Aramaic means "Our Father's revelation." It derives from combining two nouns: *Awoon* or *Evan* meaning "our Father" and *Gilyana* or *galion* denoting "revelation."

3. *Karozutha* derives from the root *krz*. It means to "preach," "declare," "make known," "announce," and "publicly celebrate." All three words are correct when translated as "gospel" but we lose the specific meaning that lies behind each word. For example, let us examine the title of the first four books of the New Testament.

The Gospels

Semitic New Testament Christian scribes use the Aramaic word *karozutha* when titling the four canonical gospels. In Aramaic the titles read as "the Preaching of Matthew, Mark, Luke, and John." The reason for this particular gospel title is that each writer presents his own view of Jesus' teaching and ministry. All four books contain Jesus' gospel. We refer to the first three—Matthew, Mark, and Luke—as synoptic gospels because they are similar. The gospel of John represents Jesus in a different pattern from the first three. He emphasizes Jesus as the Christ, the anointed and appointed one of God. This was his particular view and "take" on Jesus and his ministry.

All four writings that we call "the gospels" were written with the intention of instructing converts in their new faith before baptism. Some gospel scholars refer to them as catechisms. (A catechism is a book of religious instructions or a summary of religious principles that prepare an individual for baptism into a particular Christian faith.) These gospels prepared the early converts for their acceptance into the faith.

Jesus' Voice and the Voice of Tradition

Matthew, Mark, and Luke are a mixture of Jesus' voice and the early traditional voice of the Church. For example, Jesus' teaching was not about the "cross." His followers taught about Jesus' cross, death, and resurrection. After all, we must keep in mind that Jesus' horrendous crucifixion devastated his apostles and disciples. They were the ones who suffered the loss of their beloved master-teacher. They, because of his death and resurrection, experienced a dramatic rise in consciousness. They became transformed and now possessed spiritual sight.

Nonetheless we must also realize that it was early Christian tradition that developed the gospel of the cross and the traditional "atonement for sins." Jesus never taught the atonement gospel. This idea developed after Jesus' crucifixion:

> That the praxis [deeds or actions] of Jesus and his disciples offended the religious sensibilities not only of their fellow Jews but also of later Christians is apparent when one examines the understanding of sin and forgiveness. While the earliest Jesus' traditions eschew [avoid] any understanding of the ministry and death of Jesus in cultic terms as atonement for sins, it was precisely this interpretation

33

which soon took root in some segments of the early Christian movement. Yet such an interpretation of Jesus' death as atonement for sins is much later than is generally assumed in New Testament scholarship. The notion of atoning sacrifice does not express the Jesus movement's understanding and experience of God but is a later interpretation of the violent death of Jesus in cultic terms. The God of Jesus is not a God who demands atonement and whose wrath needs to be placated by human sacrifice or ritual. . .Although such an interpretation of the death of Jesus is soon found in early Christian theology, the death of Jesus was not a sacrifice and was not demanded by God but brought about by the Romans.[2]

Again, in Mark 16:15-16,we have another example of the developing traditional voice of the Christian Church after Jesus' death. The author attributes the following command to Jesus: "Go into all the world and preach my gospel to the whole creation. **He who believes and is baptized will be saved; and he who does not believe will be condemned**." (Bolding does not appear in the original text. I use it for emphasis.) This threat does not evince Jesus' voice but it does evidence the voice of the early expanding Church. These later followers of Jesus were recruiting new converts for their movement.

---

[2]Elisabeth Schussler Fiorenza, *In Memory of Her: A Feminist Theological Reconstruction of Christian Origins,* "The Jesus Movement as Renewal Movement Within Judaism," p. 130.See also Errico & Lamsa, *Aramaic Light on the Gospel of John,* "Did God Pay a Ransom?" pp. 50-57.

What Jesus Preached and Taught

What was Jesus' gospel? According to the message of Matthew, Mark, Luke, and some in John, Jesus announced and taught the "kingdom of God." His parables, sayings, and deeds revealed God's kingdom at work. God's reigning presence was invading his world. Jesus saw God as King (Counselor) whose kingdom was to be realized at a local level first and eventually known universally. Let us look into Mark's presentation of Jesus' gospel.

> Now after John had been arrested, Jesus came into Galilee declaring the joyful expectation of God's sovereign presence. He was saying: The time is right! God's reigning presence is here! Turn to God and have confidence in this joyful message![3]

The term kingdom may be difficult for modern readers to relate to. *Malkutha*—literally, "kingdom"—comes from the Aramaic root *mlkh*. It means to "counsel," "advise," "reign," and "rule." A king, *malka* in Aramaic, also means a counselor. *Malkutha* in Semitic languages also refers to sovereignty and in this case to God's sovereignty. According to Aramaic targumin or targums (interpretations) of that time, God's kingdom referred strictly to God. To put it more simply, the term "kingdom of God" represents God as sovereign king(ruler or counselor).

Jesus' message was God's sovereign and active presence arriving in the world. He had a vision of God that went beyond the religious limits of his day. He could perceive God as working among people, moving in and through their daily,

---

[3]Mk. 1:14-15, Aramaic Peshitta text.

routine living. Many of Jesus' parables carry this idea.

The Unobservable Kingdom

But this kingdom was not so easily discerned. When the Pharisees questioned Jesus about the appearance of God's kingdom, he replied that "God's kingdom cannot be recognized by sight. No one will be able to say: Look, here it is! Or, look it is there! It is just the opposite. God's sovereign reign is present among you!"[4] People expected God's rule to be extraordinary and spectacular. It would bring swift judgment and end the rule of Rome over Palestine. For Jesus to teach that God's reigning presence had come into the ordinary, everydayness of living was truly outrageous. How could Jesus teach such an idea when Israel was under such a harsh yoke of Roman servitude and was subject to King Herod, an Idumean and Roman puppet, ruling in Galilee?

Nonetheless, the expectation of God's kingdom was high in the hearts of the people of Jesus' generation. But there was no agreement about how God's power would present itself to Israel. The Pharisees had their own ideas about God's reign. They thought it would come about through obedience to the Mosaic purity laws. Sadducees held different opinions concerning how God would actualize the presence of the kingdom in their midst. Essenes, apocalyptic believers, and others expected that God's judgments—war, disaster, famine, pestilence, and death—would signal the beginning of God's reign and presence. Others thought that only through wisdom, steady reflection, and meditation would the kingdom make its appearance.

---

[4] Lk. 17:20-21, Aramaic Peshitta text.

Jesus held to none of the above notions concerning God's kingdom. His understanding was distinct from his contemporaries. The approach that Jesus made to the kingdom was centered in the heart of the social life of his people. For this local Galilean rabbi, God's presence was at work among children, prostitutes, tax collectors, sinners, the blind and crippled, the socially unwanted, marginalized individuals, outcasts, and the victimized. His parables, sayings, and actions revealed what he knew to be God's active presence among the people.

Jesus had a grasp of divine principles that brought life and healing to the ills of his people. His message was not about fear, threat, or sacrificial blood for the forgiveness or cleansing of sin. His gospel of the kingdom was about love, compassion, forgiveness, all-inclusiveness, and God's active presence with and among all races. This was Jesus' vision of God and his joyful message!

God's sovereignty was at hand and people all over the world would ultimately come to recognize divine rule within their own hearts and souls. This realization eventually would bring all world orders to a close; that is, it would transform them and bring the leaders of these governments to a new understanding and reverence for life.

This does not mean that Jesus upheld or championed the supremacy of a specific race or religion that was to dominate the world. He was not a racial or religious supremacist. If he held any belief in the notion of supremacy, it would be in God's sovereign, loving presence ruling our hearts and minds. There is no doubt whatsoever that Jesus taught the greatness and preeminence of God's presence. His teaching sprang directly from his inner understanding of Hebrew Scripture and from his own social and spiritual insight. Jesus was a distinctive, religious genius.

In his humanity, Jesus was a Semite, a Near Easterner, raised within the matrix of Jewish culture and ideologies that existed during his lifetime. Nonetheless, he perceived God's power and the significance of the Torah quite differently from his predecessors, contemporaries or successors. Jesus' actions and teachings explicitly represented God's activity in Israel and foreshadowed it in the coming ages. For Jesus, God's kingdom was present and active, but it was still to come in a greater way.

Recognizing God's Reign

During Jesus' time, people longed for the coming of God's power to right wrongs and to exalt the righteous. However, Jesus' parables clearly revealed that God's rule would not come as anticipated but in unusual, hidden, and unexpected ways. Jesus called not the righteous but sinners, tax collectors, and prostitutes into the kingdom. In fact, he said that *they* would enter first into the kingdom. He did not exclude the religious and the pious but they would be last to enter because they did not recognize God's kingdom. Under Jesus, the glorious kingdom of God would be populated with the unwanted, the despised, the misfits, the crippled, the beggars, the street people, and the social outcasts. How could this be? Everyone expected that God would only exalt the pious. But instead, God through Jesus was vindicating the oppressed.

Jesus' gospel of the kingdom speaks to the heart of every human being, but at the same time it overturns all false notions we may hold about ourselves and others. His teachings go against the grain of our cultural and religious beliefs. This gospel tends to destabilize the existing social and political order in any society. Once we recognize this fact, we can understand why Roman governmental powers and other world governments were persecuting this dangerous and subversive gospel. These teachings undermine all racial, religious, and societal strata that delineate between people.

The parables of Jesus tell very succinctly how God sees the human family. God alone is the true parent of all races and nations. God is the only genuine spiritual ethnic source for all races.

Most of our societal, religious, professional, and political systems create divisions between people which, in turn, create *insiders* and *outsiders*. There always seems to be the *elite* and the *common*. Not even communistic political systems are able to eliminate the lines between those *in power* and those who *work* for that *power*. In these societies people do not have things in common. They must work for the central government. They are not truly communistic in practice. There still exists the *elite* in these so-called communistic societies. Even religious circles and denominations have been unable to free themselves of this practice of *insiders* and *outsiders*, *elite* and *common*. People are segregated by belief and by social and economic strata. This gospel of the kingdom has yet to break down the iron walls of prejudice, racism, violence, separatism, and hatred that exist within our own hearts and among the peoples of all nations.

6

The Parables of Jesus
Introduction

Jesus' message was immediate and personal. He declared that God's presence was among his people. "Jesus came into Galilee declaring the joyful hope of God's sovereign counsel. He was saying: The time is right! God's reigning presence has arrived! Turn to God and trust in this joyful message!"[1] This is the gospel according to Jesus.

How Jesus Taught His Kingdom Gospel

In his ministry which consisted of parables, aphorisms, and actions, Jesus revealed different aspects of the kingdom. He constantly told short and poignant narratives. Often, he would tell a tale in just one verse. Some New Testament scholars refer to his one-verse parables as "one liners."

Jesus, through his parables, brings us in close communication with his religious imagination and his teaching about God's kingdom. His parables are stories that act as referents for *God's sovereign ruling (counseling) presence*. These parables refer directly to God's loving royal presence and activity in our world.

For modern readers of the New Testament, this twofold idea, "kingdom of God," appears as an outdated expression. We

---

[1]Mk. 1:14-15, Aramaic Peshitta text.

seldom think in terms of kings and queens, or monarchs of great realms. There are other biblical scholars who suggest that Jesus used the term "God's sovereignty" in contrast to Roman sovereignty.

Many New Testament authorities teach that the authentic voice of the Galilean teacher did not moralize, condemn, or harangue. However, this does not mean that Jesus was not an ethical teacher. And according to these scholars, Jesus messages did not center in or around his own person such as we find recorded in the gospel of John. Interestingly, it was the scribe (writer) of John's gospel who created Jesus' long speeches and discourses.

According to the synoptic gospels (Matthew, Mark, Luke), Jesus taught in parables and concise sayings and not in mono-logues. And his own person was not the focus of his ministry. His major theme was the Kingdom of God. He did not preach about himself. In John's gospel the focus changes to eternal life and on the man Jesus as the Christ. However, Matthew's gospel tells us that "Jesus spoke all these things to the multitudes **in parables** and **without parables** he did not speak to them."[2]

Jesus as Poet and Humorist

Aramaic and Hebrew speech is exceedingly poetic. But the poetry is not according to the English sense of verse and rhyme. Semitic poetry does not follow our Western poetic standards. Its style of writing and spoken form have a set rhythm and repetition along with contrasting and complementary parallelism. Undoubtedly, Jesus always spoke as a poet when telling his

---

[2]Mt. 13:34, Aramaic Peshitta text.

stories, many of which were ironic and humorous. He formed words in a specific way for his listeners that created a new sense of reality about God's kingdom.

Greek and English versions of the gospels do retain the Semitic, poetic structure of Jesus' narratives. However, we need to realize that the gospels contain adaptations and translations of his parables. Although the synoptic gospel writers have edited and interpreted many of Jesus' stories within their gospel texts, Jesus' message is clearly present. In other words, we do not have the exact words of Jesus in his stories. What the gospels do retain are his central ideas and paradigms which are present in the retelling of his narratives. These structures maintain Jesus' poetic style, wit, and humor. As a general rule, all gospel interpretations of Jesus' short stories are not his voice. This does not mean that these interpretations put on the lips of Jesus are invalid or unimportant. Through these explanations we can comprehend the growing and expanding traditional, early Christian voice.

What Is a Parable?

Before we venture any deeper into our topic, we need to understand the meaning of the word "parable." Our English word "parable" comes from the Greek term *parabole*. *Para* means "parallel" or "alongside." The second half of the word derives from the Greek term *ballein* and signifies to "throw," "cast," or "place." A parable, then, is a story we place alongside something else to help clarify its meaning. Jesus' parables help us to understand and perceive God's kingdom—that is, God's gracious and loving presence.

In Hebrew the word is *mashal* and in Aramaic the term is

pelatha. Both these Semitic words carry the same root idea of "it is like," "similar," or "it is compared to." *Mashal* and *pelatha* may also translate into English as "parable," "proverb," "allegory," "illustration," "riddle," and "similitude."

Teaching and carrying on a conversation in parables, proverbs, riddles, and illustrations is characteristic of a Semite. Wise men, wazirs, court officials, rabbis, prophets, teachers, and politicians always used parables in their debates and speeches. Merchants and clients, while bargaining, often mention a few parables.

Near Eastern musicians sing parables, proverbs, and riddles as they play their instruments. "I will incline my ear to parables: I will sing my proverbs upon the harp."[3] Speaking in parables was a common way of communicating between Near Eastern Semites and it remains so to this very day. This kind of speech is very precious to them. It is poetic, mystical, and social.

Parables are extremely important if one is to comprehend the power and meaning of God's sovereign guidance. Through Jesus' parables we begin to perceive God's working in the world. Although there exists much violence, hatred, prejudice, and injustice in our world, we can gain a new perspective of ourselves and our world from Jesus' narratives. The need to transcend our present condition and world system is vital to everyone. All humanity is at the crossroads. No longer can we continue to live with the crime and violence that are so prevalent today. Jesus' kingdom message provides us an antidote for our present ills or for any further maladies that may develop in the future.

---

[3]Ps. 49:4, Aramaic Peshitta text.

Jesus the Parabler

Jesus was a parablist—that is, a teller of parables. He constantly told concise and compelling stories. Some of his tales were exhilarating (Matthew 13:54) and others were offensive (Mark 12:12). People usually responded to his narratives because they were also enlightening (Mark 4:30), confusing (Matthew 15:15), a threat to temporal powers (Luke 12:1-21), and bringing realization of God's reality (Mark 4:30). Jesus' parables also destroy the divisive and imaginary *insider* versus *outsider* mentality and boundaries that religious, cultural, racial, and political powers usually create (Luke 10:30-35).

His message was positive and practical. Through his parables we learn that God engages with people now. God identifies with common, ordinary folk, and the misfits of society. Jesus taught that God is in solidarity with people. God is with us at all times, in sickness, sorrow, everydayness of life, and in death. We usually recoil from the ordinary, common, and unacceptable in our particular society. But that is precisely where God's presence is active. God is present with the just and the unjust, the good and the wicked. God is no respecter of persons. According to Matthew's gospel, Jesus makes this point very explicit. (See Matthew 5:43-48.)

First Century Palestine

In first century Palestine, certain religious traditions and attitudes—along with apocalyptic expectations—were prevalent. People thought of God as some far-off, mysterious, awesome, and fearsome deity who would come with swift judgment to punish wicked people and nations. Here are just a few of the popular widespread notions concerning the end of the world at that time. (This brief religious summation of certain attitudes is by no means a complete picture.)

1. There was an apocalyptic belief stemming from such books as Daniel and Enoch that through God's judgment a redeemer would transform their present age into an age of holiness.

2. This redeemer would open the way for another world or age that was to come.

3. Divine punishment would create a moral world.

4. Evil comes from a supernatural world of fallen angels, and this evil is imposed from outside humankind. God must defeat this evil.

5. Some believed that the only way one could cope with the world was with the wisdom of ages past.

Jesus differed from all these ideas and the religious traditions of his time. His parables turned the major religious belief systems and notions upside down. This prophet's voice was distinct from those who came before him and from those who followed him. Jesus of Nazareth was totally unique and one of a kind. There is no doubt that many of Jesus' parables and short "cutting-edge" sayings provoked the cry for his death. (See Luke 20:9-20).

Not All Parables Originate with Jesus

New Testament scholars tell us that the synoptic gospel writers (Matthew, Mark, and Luke) attribute approximately forty parables to Jesus. However some modern interpreters claim that only twenty-five to twenty-eight of these parables originated with Jesus. The beginning Christian traditional voice created at least twelve or fifteen of the forty parables present in the three synoptic gospels.

The early followers of Jesus placed these twelve or fifteen parables on his lips. They formulated them to meet the needs and challenges that the growing Christian communities were facing in the first century. In the ancient Near East this was a common practice, especially in a culture that relied heavily on oral tradition.

The Parable of the Ten Virgins

Let's take for example the parable of the Ten Virgins recorded in Matthew 25:1-13. This short story was developed to warn the Christian community about the delayed but soon returning presence of their Christ. The community was to be watchful, waiting, preparing, doing their master's service until he should return. If one were not watching, waiting, and preparing for the master's return, that one would be thrown into *outer darkness* where there would be *weeping and gnashing of teeth.*[4]

In this parable we are dealing with the notion of *insiders* versus *outsiders*, or *who will be in* and *who will be out.* Thus, the early disciples created the story of the Ten Virgins. How do we know they composed this narrative and placed it on Jesus' lips? We know this to be the early Christian traditional voice because Jesus' short stories invariably taught an all-inclusive kingdom, eliminating boundaries, not building them. The early believers, through this parable, were attempting to encourage their converts to faithful service to Jesus. They were not to be

---

[4]An Aramaic idiom meaning deep anguish and regret.

discouraged because their master (the Christ) delayed his return.

The Original Setting of the Parables

When Jesus' parables originally circulated orally among the early followers of his movement, these stories were without a specified, historical setting. They were passed on by word of mouth as independent units of speech—that is, without a context. We know from historical research that Jesus was interested in only one matter and that was God's now active presence among the people. This was his purpose! Therefore, his parables related and focused on the theme of the kingdom. The synoptic gospel writers furnish us with their own settings for Jesus' parables. This framing of the parables, in Hebrew, is called *nimshal*.

In the ancient world it was also a common practice to add short explanatory comments after riddles, fables, parables, and other figures of speech:

> The simplest way for the synoptic writers to interpret the parables of Jesus was to append a brief explanation, summarizing their understanding of the parable's meaning. These concluding applications are usually introduced with the adverb "thus," or "so." An example of a brief application after a parable with the "so" formula is Matthew 18:35: "So also my heavenly Father will do to every one of you, if you do not forgive your brother from your heart." The fact that Matthew and Luke have each provided a different interpretation of the Lost Sheep shows that these applications are secondary:
> *So it is not the will of my Father who is in heaven that one of these little ones should perish.* (Mt. 18:14)

Just so, I tell you, there will be more joy in heaven over one sinner who repents than over ninety-nine righteous persons who need no repentance. (Lk. 15:7)[5]

Craig L. Blomberg, in his research on current trends among scholars on the parables of Jesus, makes this comment:

One of the more straightforward conclusions that emerges from both Stern and Johnston, and the data they analyze, is that the rabbinic *mashal* [parable] regularly divides into two parts—the *mashal* proper and the *nimshal*, an appended explanation which usually identifies, or enables an allegorical equation of the main characters, objects and events of the *mashal* with God, Israel and various events in her history. Although plentiful already in the Tannaitic era, the *nimshalim* became a standardized feature of the Amoraic times. Stern suggests a growing development in this direction, which makes it natural to place Jesus' parables, with their only occasionally explicit allegorical "expansions" (The Sower and the Wheat and Tares), but with their regular framing material, in a time when the *nimshal* had not achieved standard form. But all this suggests that, whether from Jesus or the tradition, such explanatory material fell well within the range of what Jewish interpreters expected the *mashal* to do, ought not be viewed as misrepresenting original intent, and cannot be jettisoned in the interpretive process.[6]

---

[5]Lane C. McGaughy, *A Short History of Parable Interpretation*, p. 231, (THE FORUM, Vol. 8, Nos. 3/4, Sept./Dec. 1992).

[6]See Bruce Chilton & Craig A. Evans, *Studying the Historical Jesus: Evaluations of the State of Current Research,* "The Parables of Jesus: Current Trends and Needs in Research," p. 235, Brill, 1998.

Let us now take, for example, the parable of Jesus known as the Good Samaritan. Biblical interpreters have titled this short story as "The Good Samaritan." Jesus never gave any titles to his brief narratives. We find the so-called Good Samaritan parable in Luke 10:30-35.

Most New Testament authorities agree that Jesus told this narrative. However, the verses that introduce the telling of the Good Samaritan, Luke 10:25-29, have a particular interpretation which differed from Jesus' original theme. Let us recall that Jesus' prime objective in telling parables was to interpret the kingdom—God's sovereign presence.

Thus, when Luke included the parable in his writings, he framed it with an edited and reshaped scene borrowed from the gospel of Matthew.[7] (See Mt. 19:16, 19 and 22:34-40.) Luke did this to answer the question, "Who is my neighbor?" "So, who, of these three, as it seems to you, was the neighbor to him who fell into the hands of the bandits? Then he replied: He who had compassion on him. Jesus answered him: Now, you also go and do the same."[8] Luke also wanted to emphasize the idea that one must *practice* the teaching and *not just hear* it; one must *do* and *not just listen*. Although Luke's gospel has a good point, this

---

[7]Other NT experts claim that Mt. has reshaped the story from Mk. 12:28-24. If one concurs with the Q hypothesis of the Synoptic gospels, then Mt. has copied Mk. and Lk also has copied Mk. However, I do not adhere to this hypothesis but follow the notion that Mt. was the original gospel and not Mk. This is based on the work suggested by a team of scholars who go beyond the Q hypothesis. See Allan J. McNicol, with David L. Dungan and David B. Peabody, *Luke's Use of Matthew, Beyond the Q impasse — A Demonstration by the Research Team of the International Institute for Gospel Studies*.

[8]Lk. 10:36-37, Aramaic Peshitta text.

49

probably was not Jesus' perspective of the parable.

According to the story, a lawyer or scribe did not like Jesus' answer to the question he had asked. So, he tried to justify himself by asking, "Who is my neighbor?" Once Luke devised his own setting with this question, the parable's initial meaning became muted. Nonetheless, just because Luke changed its direction does not make his interpretation of the parable invalid.

Luke's interpretation is an excellent lesson. It teaches what it means to truly respond as a compassionate neighbor and do good, despite the fact that Jesus' original point became dormant. In the following chapter we begin with the Good Samaritan parable.

7

The Parables of Jesus
Part One

Jesus told parables to help people discern God's kingdom. Let us recall that the "kingdom" represented God's presence or the reality of God now present in and through life's "every-dayness." God was with Israel but in a manner that the people had not imagined. It took Jesus' powerful Semitic imagination to awaken the hearts and minds of the populace of Palestine.

A Few Things to Consider

We need to consider a few points before we begin with Jesus' short fictional narratives:

1. Jesus told these stories; therefore, they were not written short stories.

2. Jesus always had his hearers in mind. So he knew he would have listener response.

3. As far as we know, Jesus never titled his tales nor did he interpret them.

4. He told these parables in a certain manner so that his audience would remember them. They were about family life at home, in the village, and in the city. He also composed fictional stories about farming, about masters and their servants, and a single story about life beyond this one. As he related these parables, he used a great deal of repetition, setting characters and things in pairs or in threes (mostly threes). He used humor,

irony, exaggeration, and graphic intensiveness. In an oral culture, all the above styles of telling a story were important and served to help the people remember what they had heard.[1] I will explain only a few outstanding parables of Jesus.

The Good Samaritan

First, I will present my translation of the parable from the ancient Aramaic Peshitta text. I have renamed most of Jesus' parables. With these innovative titles, I have attempted to capture fresh insight into the narratives by using humorous and sometimes double meanings behind most of the new titles. As the explanation of the parable becomes clear, the reader will come to understand the humorous or double meaning titles I invented.

Then, I will repeat the story one line, or a few lines, at a time, explaining customs and other details of the story. There are many connotations to Jesus' parables. The interpretation I offer is only one of many insights into the kingdom that one can glean from Jesus' stories. In other words, I make no claim that the interpretation I present is the one and only explanation. Jesus' parables are multi-faceted like a diamond and, therefore, they can have many interpretations.

There is another point we must keep in mind. All his narratives were originally *told* and *not written*. There were no set verses in a particular chapter as we now have them in the three synoptic gospels. People heard these stories so they were

---

[1]For a detailed modern study on the parables, see Bernard Brandon Scott, *Hear Then the Parable: A Commentary on the Parables of Jesus.*

impacted on emotional and intellectual levels. They could not remain neutral listening to these stories. Contrastingly, we read these stories and do not hear them in their Semitic cultural background. All that remains for us is their literary structure. What is missing is the manner in which these tales were spoken. Jesus' emphasis, gestures, voice inflections, and emotional projections are not there. I have attempted to translate the literary story as if one were hearing it. The double space between certain lines is a break in the narrative that shows the suspense Jesus was building.

The Unexpected Hero

A man was traveling from Jerusalem to Jericho.
Suddenly robbers attacked him,
stripped him,
and left him half dead.
Then they went away.

And by chance,
a priest was traveling down that road,
saw him,
and passed by.
So then a Levite also came
and reached the same place,
saw him,
and passed by.

Now a man, a Samaritan,
while he was traveling,
came where he was,
saw him,

53

and had compassion on him.
So he went to him,
dressed his wounds,
having poured wine and oil on them.
Then he mounted him on his donkey,
brought him to an inn,
and attended to him.

On the following day,
early in the morning,
he took out two denareen,
and gave them to the innkeeper.
He told him: Take good care of him.
Whatever you may need in addition,
when I come back,
I will repay you.[2]

All cultures, religious and racial orders, governments, and so forth, have always maintained a certain hierarchic order with invisible social and mental boundary lines. In the ancient world for example, there were Greeks and Barbarians, Jews and Gentiles. Biblical Israel also maintained a hierarchy among its own people. A quote from the Mishnah[3] shows and establishes this hierarchic system. "A priest precedes a Levite, a Levite an Israelite, and an Israelite a bastard, a bastard a Nathin, a Nathin a proselyte, and a proselyte a freed slave and so forth."

---

[2]Lk. 10:30-35.

[3]The Mishnah is the written compilation of orally transmitted legal teachings covering all aspects of Jewish law, arranged in six orders that, in turn, are divided into tractates, executed by Judah ha-Nasi, around 200 C.E. Palestine.

When Jesus related his parable, he jolted his listeners by not following the usual hierarchic formula. He begins his story with the appearance of a priest, then a Levite, but he surprises his audience with a non-Israelite hero. This was a shocker! Almost immediately he begins breaking down social strata that religious notions and traditions had built. This simple but explosive story challenged his audience. How does this apply to the kingdom of God?

An Explanation

"A man was traveling from Jerusalem to Jericho." The road from the Holy City to Jericho is about seventeen miles and it is extremely dangerous. It passes through mostly desert and rocky hills. Jesus' listeners felt the tension in the story right away. They knew that this road was notorious for mugging and highway robbery. So the next sequence of events in the tale was no surprise to them.

"Robbers attacked him, stripped him, and left him half-dead. Then they went away." When the thieves took his clothes, they left the unfortunate fellow without any identification. In the Near East, clothes help identify an individual. Clothes tell about a person's class, religion, and from what village or clan he or she originates. These robbers had so badly beaten the Israelite victim, he appeared as dead. (We assume the victim was an Israelite because Jesus was speaking to a largely Jewish audience.)

"And by chance, a priest was traveling down that road, saw him, and passed by. So then a Levite came and reached that same place, saw him, and passed by." Interestingly, Jericho was a hometown for priests and Levites. Thus, it was no accident

that Jesus had a priest and Levite traveling down that same road.

According to Levitical law, a priest or a Levite must not touch a bloody or dead body. "The LORD said to Moses: Speak to the priests, the sons of Aaron, and say to them: None shall defile himself for any [dead] person among his kin, except for the relatives that are closest to him: his mother, his father, his son, his daughter, and his brother."[4] In Israel the dead were unclean—therefore, untouchable. In Numbers 19:11, anyone touching a corpse will be unclean for seven days. So the priest and Levite were religiously and Levitically correct to pass by the victim.

If Jesus had any Pharisees, priests, or Levites among his listeners, they would have decidedly approved of the clergy's action. But the common folk definitely would have disapproved of their behavior. Where was their compassion? Undoubtedly, Jesus must have had a mixed response to this parable, at least up to this point. Probably the majority of his listeners were in complete sympathy with the beaten and robbed Israelite thrown on the side of the road. This story needs a hero. Somebody has to help the pathetic victim who fell prey to the highway criminals. But the surprise element in the story is yet to come.

*"Now a man. . .a **Samaritan**, while he was traveling came where he was. . . saw him. . .and **had compassion on him**."* Undoubtedly, this part of the story agitated nearly everyone's racial and religious sensibilities. At first, when Jesus introduced the Samaritan as the new player in his parable, people might have thought that the Samaritan would finish what the robbers had not done. But instead, Jesus has a Samaritan fill the role as the hero of the plot. The Samaritan had compassion on the Israelite. This parable was troublesome because his audience

---

[4]Lev. 21:1-2, The New JPS translation from Hebrew.

56

could not identify with anyone in the story. How could this be—a hero was a non-Israelite? But worst of all—a Samaritan?

The Samaritans

The Samaritans and the Jews had long been enemies. This history originated at the time of the rebuilding of Solomon's temple and the return of the Jewish exiles from Chaldea (Babylonia). We need to start with Samaria, the capital of the kingdom of Israel—the Ten [northern] Tribes of Israel. This does not include the Southern kingdom of Judah. Its capital was Jerusalem. King Omri about 880 B.C.E. founded Samaria. The Assyrians in 721 B.C.E. captured the entire Northern kingdom of Israel, deported its people and resettled the territory with pagans from other parts of their empire (2 Kings 18:9-12 and chapter 17).

According to Jewish tradition, the Samaritans were the descendants of these settlers. We do not know the exact date when the Samaritans became a separate religious sect with a temple of their own on Mt. Gerizim. However, most scholars favor the fourth century B.C.E. Evidently, Jesus had some sympathy for this group of people. This is shown through his parable of the "Good Samaritan" and the story of the Ten Lepers (Luke 17:11-19). Nevertheless, Jesus himself instructed the twelve apostles not to enter any town of the Samaritans, but rather to go to the lost sheep of the house of Israel (Matthew 10:5-6).

The Samaritans do not derive their name from any geographical designation, but rather from the term *samerim*, "keeper [of the law]." John 4:9 informs readers that the Jews had no dealings with the Samaritans. These Samaritans felt they were a special chosen group and called themselves "the sons of light." They criticized the Jerusalem temple, and they did not celebrate Purim or Hanukkah.

Samaritans also adapted their own special edited Torah but did not accept the books of the prophets. They were a religious community that developed independently of the spiritual leadership of Jerusalem among a people who were, for cultural and historical reasons, alienated from the Jews and could not maintain friendly relations. There is a proverbial saying about this hostility between Jew and Samaritan. "He that eats the bread of the Samaritans is like to one who eats the flesh of swine."[5]

The Continuation of the Parable

"*So he went up to him and dressed his wounds, having poured wine and oil on them.*" Near Easterners used oil, wine, and honey as medicines. In the story the wine is for preventing infection and the oil is for soothing the skin. "*Then he mounted him on his donkey, brought him to an inn, and attended to him. Now on the following day, early in the morning, he took out two denareen[6] and gave them to the innkeeper and told him: Take good care of him. Whatever you may spend in addition, when I come back, I'll make it good.*" By now Jesus' startled audience was aghast. Jesus had made his point.

---

[5]Bernard Brandon Scott, *Hear Then the Parable: A Commentary on the Parables of Jesus*, "Who's That Masked Man?" p. 197.

[6]A denaray was a silver coin. One denaray was the accepted salary for a day's work.

A Meaning for us

God's kingdom—that is, God's sovereign presence—subverts all hierarchic order of any present or future religious and political systems. In this kingdom there are no lines of demarcation—no boundaries—nor is there any social strata. No one is greater than or above anyone else.

Jesus made a Samaritan the savior. This hero does not convert to any accepted religious belief so that he may become an acceptable hero and savior. He remains a Samaritan. Also, through this parable, Jesus ruined the apocalyptic, destructive vision and notion of one's ultimate victory over enemies, religious or nonreligious.

According to Jesus' parable, the enemy has compassion, heals, and cares for an Israelite. And the poor, robbed Israelite had to be touched, cleaned, and placed on a donkey by a man who was considered culturally and religiously unclean. Then he was provided with room and board and clothing by this contemptible and hated enemy. The bludgeoned and mugged Israelite had no choice. He had to receive help from the Samaritan.

All racial and religious boundaries have broken down in this story. The only ones who could not break through their religious chains were the priest and the Levite. Levitical principles prevented them from showing compassion and giving aid. Powerful religious laws held them prisoners.

The Samaritan crossed over all boundaries, showed compassion and aided the nearly dead man. He didn't inquire to see if the man was worth saving. Quietly the little bit of life that was left in the battered man was calling for help. The Samaritan was able to hear this life calling him. He was not afraid to aid this needy human being on the roadside. The despised Samaritan transcended his racial and religious beliefs and helped the Israelite. This is God's sovereign presence at work! This is how Jesus taught God's kingdom.

A Great Banquet

With this parable, Jesus changed another invalid idea and tradition about God's kingdom. We know this parable as "The Great Supper or Feast." It appears only in the gospels of Matthew and Luke.

Again, some New Testament experts believe that the Matthew version of this parable (Matthew 22:2-14) underwent heavy editing, so much so that the original intent has completely disappeared. Matthew interprets the parable for his own teaching purposes. This was a common practice for all three gospel writers. These scholars claim that Matthew's version of the parable itself does not carry the authentic voice of Jesus.

Contrastingly, they believe that Luke's version retains Jesus' initial structure for this parable or at least something close to it.[7] Luke evidently had other sources for this story and did not rely on Matthew. Interestingly, the gospel of Thomas has a similar parable.[8] "The similarity of this Lukan parable with the one in the Gospel of Thomas may suggest that the author of the Gospel of Thomas was familiar with the same story to which Luke had access, or that the author of the Gospel of Thomas was

---

[7]See Bernard Brandon Scott, *Jesus, Symbol-Maker for the Kingdom*, "A Great Banquet" pp. 32-38 and *Hear Then the Parable*, pp. 3-78. John R. Donahue, S.J. *The Gospel in Parable*, "How Does a Parable Mean?" pp. 1-27. Robert W. Funk, *Parables and Presence*.

[8]Gospel of Thomas 64.

literarily dependent on Luke for this story." [9]

The following is my translation of Luke 14:16-24 from the Aramaic Peshitta text without the setting that the evangelist created. I have renamed this parable:

A Party of Nobodies

A man gave a banquet,
and invited many.
Now at the time of the banquet,
he sent his servant to tell those who
had been invited:
Look! Everything is ready for you. Come!

Every single one of them began to make excuses.
The first one said:
I have just bought a field,
and I have to go and check it out.
I beg you to let me be excused.

Another said:
I have just bought five yoke of oxen,
and I have to go and inspect them.
So, I beg you to allow me to be excused.

Yet another said:
I have just taken a wife,
and because of this,
I cannot come.

---

[9]*Luke's Use of Matthew, Beyond the Q Impasse*, "The Eschatological Banquet" p. 211.

Now then, the servant returned
and reported to his master these things.

Then the master of the house became furious.
He said to his servant:
Go out quickly into the streets
and marketplaces of the city.
Bring back the poor, the afflicted,
the maimed, and the blind.
(So that my house may be filled.)[10]

Commentary

"A man threw a party and invited many. Now at the time of the party, he sent his servant to tell those who had been invited: Look here! Everything is ready for you. Come!" In the Near East, one must have an abundance of food not only to serve the guests but to show one's wealth as well. Evidently, this was a wealthy man because he had the means to put on a huge party. All the invitations, by word of mouth through the servant, had been issued. Now everything was set for the feasting, so the servant was sent out again according to custom to tell the guests that all was ready.

"Then one after another began to make excuses. The first one said: I have bought a field. Now I must go and check it out. I beg you to let me be excused." In the Near East, when a man purchases a field he usually places a deposit on the land. Then the seller and purchaser agree on a specific time to inspect the

---

[10]Many scholars suggest that Jesus did not include this final line in his narrative.

field. If the purchaser fails to check the land during this specified time, he either loses the deposit or he must pay the balance that they agreed upon.

"Another said: I have just bought five yoke of oxen and I must go and inspect them. So, I beg you to allow me to be excused." Again, in the Near East oxen and horses are purchased on a trial basis. The buyer is free to return the animals if they are not suited for his purpose. Usually the animal seller and the purchaser must both be present when the animals are inspected. Also, witnesses must be present during this tryout period.

"Yet another said: I have just taken a wife and because of this I cannot come." According to Jewish law, men are excused from going to war if they are about to marry (Deuteronomy 24:5). In Islamic countries when a man marries, he is exempt from the military for a year and from any other governmental obligations which would take him away from his newly wedded wife. This law will also excuse the man if he should take a second wife the following year.

But as far as the parable is concerned, all three excuses were a charade. Why? Because all of them had been invited before any purchase of property, animals or the taking of a wife. They all had received and accepted invitations when the servant had first announced the dinner party. They were snubbing the host who was giving the great banquet.

These guests simply did not want to attend the special feast. Their lame apologies were insincere and the servant and the host knew it. The second appearance of the servant at their homes served only as a call that all was ready for them to participate in the celebration. These guests had slighted and insulted the servant's master and gracious host. However, the master's response to this social outrage was even more surprising!

"Then the master of the house became furious. So he commanded his servant: Quickly, go out into the streets and market places of the city, and bring back the poor, the afflicted, the maimed and blind." Immediately, the servant obeyed his master's orders and brought in the outcasts. Although the dining room was now teeming with the "poor, afflicted, maimed, blind, and street people," the host wanted more guests. So he sent his servant out into the highways and byways looking for additional people to attend. He ordered his servant to "urge" the people to come. This insistence on attendance is typical Near Eastern etiquette. Usually one must "urge" an individual no less than seven times.

Near Eastern Hospitality

Alesso, in Aramaic, means "to urge" and "to insist." An Easterner as a host will almost beg his guests to attend with sayings such as "You must come to my house. By the head of my son, I would not eat if you are not present." "My house is your house, and I am your servant." They do this because no party is a success without crowds of people and a long waiting line of guests outside. With such a smashing attendance the popularity and reputation of the host spreads throughout the town. In certain areas of the Near East, the host will give presents to his guests after the feast is over. The host of this great banquet wanted his house overflowing with guests.

There is some of Jesus' humor in this story, although it is sad and pathetic for the host. Can you imagine a wealthy man's house filled with poverty-stricken street people, the lame, the afflicted, and the blind at his sumptuous table? These people would not have the refinement of those who were originally invited. What must have taken place when they were dining?

When the master invited all these despised and unfortunate people into his home, he lost his honor. But, by the same token, when he opened the banquet to society's outcasts, he was mocking the ones who were previously invited. The rich man identifies himself with social and economic rejects—that is, street people, the poor, the lame, and the blind. He had a dinner party full of nobodies. What a banquet!

Jesus' reveals God's kingdom in a new way. God's presence is with the lower class, poor, and outcasts. Jesus declared: "Delighted are the poor for God's kingdom belongs to you."[11] And again in Matthew, "Delighted are those who surrender to God [poor in spirit] for heaven's sovereign rule belongs to you."[12] God's sovereign presence appears in the most outlandish places and with the most inconceivable people. Society's religiously admissible and professionally acceptable decline the invitation to celebrate God's presence. Again, we discover God in the oddest places.

A Discreditable Judge

With this next parable, the gospel of Luke frames Jesus' story around the idea that one must persevere in prayer. In other words, if a corrupt judge will eventually respond and answer a destitute widow's plea, how much more will our gracious heavenly Father grant our prayer requests. The truth is that Jesus told parables so that his listeners would perceive God's kingdom in a new way.

---

[11]Lk. 6:20, Aramaic Peshitta text.

[12]Mt. 5:3, Aramaic Peshitta text.

We always need to keep in mind that Jesus' theme was God's sovereignty—God's active presence in our lives. Luke's theme and interpretation of the parable is about prayer and vindication, that one must not lose heart when praying. He does not have God's kingdom as his theme at all. He had a special lesson within his gospel story to emphasize. His approach proved valuable for his listeners and the Christian community. The entire setting for the parable within this gospel is Chapter 18:1-7. We are working only with the narrative itself and not with Luke's interpretation.

Here Comes the Pest

There was a judge in a certain city,
who neither had any fear of God
nor had he any respect
for human beings.

Now there was a widow in that city.
She was constantly coming to him,
saying: Vindicate me from my adversary!
But he was not willing to for a long time.

But afterwards he said to himself:
Though I do not revere God
nor respect human beings,
yet, because this widow causes me trouble,
I will vindicate her.
so that she may not be constantly
coming and badgering me.

An Explanation

The parable's magistrate was a corrupt judge. In Israel, judges were to revere God, for by so doing, they would comply with God's law and practice justice for all. "You will provide, from among all the people, capable men who revere God, honest men who detest bribes and duplicity."[13]

Widows must be respected and cared for. Israel's law protected widows, orphans, and foreigners. "You will not abuse any foreigner nor oppress him. For you were strangers in the land of Egypt. You will not ill-treat any widow or orphan. If you abuse them, and they pray before me, I will surely hear their prayer; and my anger will burn, and I will slay you with the sword. Then your wives will become widows and your children fatherless."[14] Israel's prophets cried out against injustices done to widows, orphans, and foreigners.

Near Eastern Judges

According to Dr. George M. Lamsa, who was from northern Iraq, Near Easterners regard many of their judges as cruel and dishonest. He says that they usually classify them with "publicans and sinners." No matter what kind of charitable donations a judge may make as a churchman or how he may help the poor, people, generally, look upon him rather warily. They suspect him of practicing injustice.

Most Near Eastern judges are hesitant about taking cases for widows and poor people. They usually try to excuse themselves

---

[13]Ex. 18:21, Aramaic Peshitta text. See also 2 Chron. 19:6-7.

[14]Ex. 22:21-24, Aramaic Peshitta text. See also Dt. 24:17-18.

by saying they are in poor health or that they are suffering from case overload. Others may promise aid but do not follow through with their promises. Nevertheless, the poor and widows consistently keep returning to the judge's home, begging and badgering him for a hearing.

In those ancient days and even in some areas of the Near East today, judges did not and do not receive any salary for their services. Thus, it is easy for them to accept bribes because they need the money to live. People, being aware of this situation, send their bribes a few days before they visit a particular judge. Many judges can tell when a poor person has come to their homes because that individual has not sent any payment ahead of time. A servant will usually greet these petitioners with the sad news that the judge is too busy and cannot be bothered with them at this time. Many judges feel it would lose too much of their time to work with widows and the poor. At times, judges are forced to help these needy petitioners.[15]

Jesus' Humor in the Tale

The magistrate that Jesus describes is totally shameless and does not care about honor. But because the widow kept coming and pestering him for a very long time, he finally gave in and provided the justice she needed. Jesus' humor is in the irony of the story. This judge who was not afraid of God nor of any human being, nonetheless, finally comes to fear this poor widow. Imagine, a corrupt judge who was an outlaw magistrate fearing no human being or God Almighty was afraid of the

---

[15]See Errico & Lamsa, *Aramaic Light on the Gospels of Mark and Luke*, "The Godless Judge," pp. 237-239.

weakest member of society. Again, Jesus surprises us with a simple story that carries a profound message.

God's kingdom is ever present, constantly coming and wearing down any resistance. God's presence doesn't come with a great display of awesome power but like a nuisance that won't go away. This kingdom pesters us until we open to its power and grace. The ever-present kingdom will keep badgering humanity until humankind recognizes and acknowledges its presence within their hearts. God's ruling presence never gives up on anyone!

8

The Parables of Jesus
Part Two

Jesus grew up in a northern Palestinian village, in the small town of Nazareth. So it was only natural that he would compose his parables about the environment of a Galilean hamlet, using common ordinary facets of daily life to convey his idea of God's kingdom.

His parables negated and overturned much of the religious traditions and notions of the time. Many of his "one-liner" parables carried an enormous impact for his listeners. Often New Testament scholars refer to Jesus' "one-liner" stories as "proverbial parables." This next parable is one of Jesus' very short stories. We usually refer to this brief story as "the Parable of the Leaven" because Jesus opens his "one-liner" with "the kingdom of heaven is like leaven." I have renamed the parable:

The Covert Kingdom

Heaven's sovereignty is like leaven. . .
which a woman took and hid. . .
in three measures of flour. . .
until all had risen.[1]

---

[1]Mt. 13:33, Aramaic Peshitta text. Matthew uses the term "heaven" euphemistically for "God." One may translate the phrase as "God's sovereignty."

The Setting

Before Herod's soldiers had seized and arrested John the Baptist, he had been announcing that God's anger was about to erupt (Matthew 3:7, Luke 3:7, 9). At that time, many Palestinians were anticipating God's swift and wrathful judgments to come upon the land, wipe out Herodian rule and displace Roman authority with God's authority. With this parable Jesus struck a powerful blow to misleading expectations of God's sovereign presence.

Key Words

Three key words that help unlock the parable's meaning are "leaven" (yeast), "woman," and "hid." A woman was preparing to bake bread. So she put the leaven in "three measures (50 pounds) of flour until all had risen." Jesus uses the amount of flour (50 pounds) as an exaggeration. This makes the story border on the humorous.

In addition to the humor, the parable also contains a sharp affront to the religious cultural notions about women. Jesus' audience realizes this surprising barb when he compares God's sovereignty (kingdom) to a woman doing an ordinary, mundane action of preparing bread for baking. How could Jesus compare God's great and all-powerful sovereign presence to a woman? And not only did he compare the kingdom to a woman, but to a woman doing a household womanly thing. No doubt, this must have been quite a shock to his listeners.

Jesus next eye-opener is the term "leaven" and his use of the expression "hiding" or "burying" the leaven in "three measures" of flour. In preparing flour for baking bread, fermentation is necessary. It is a process of corruption and putrefaction in the mass of dough. Jesus says that the woman "hid" or "buried" the leaven. Once the leaven is hidden in the dough no one can see what it is doing deep in the flour. It is completely concealed. It is a covert operation especially in 50 pounds of flour.

God's kingdom or sovereign presence reverses what is normally acceptable. Usually religious rules and thinking create a division between what is profane and what is sacred. According to Jesus, God's presence acts covertly, undermining present cultural and religious perspectives. God's active presence is secretly at work. It doesn't work in the open.

Jesus compares the kingdom to fermentation, corrupting old ideas so that what is truly valid may appear. We can easily miss God's kingdom because it works in a hidden manner. This kingdom's operation is not obvious to human awareness. "God's sovereignty cannot be recognized by sight. No one will be able to say: Look, here it is! Or, Look, it is there! It is just the opposite! God's sovereignty is present among you."[2]

Fermenting Power

God's presence appears in its own way and not according to our acceptable norms. It doesn't come with great wrath and judgment but like a woman hiding "leaven" in 50 pounds of flour. When the dough rises then it is ready for baking. Kingdom principles must ferment in us, removing all barriers that separate us from God, ourselves, and others.

There are no levels of status in God's kingdom. Division

---

[2]Lk. 17:20-21, Aramaic Peshitta text.

and separation are not part of the divine presence. Sin means "to miss the mark." So any notions—including rigid, religious, legalistic, doctrinal absolutes—that separate us from God, ourselves, and the human family, are the very essence and meaning of sin—"missing the mark."

We must remember that God is spirit and love. According to John's gospel, Jesus says to the Samaritan woman: "For God is spirit. Those who worship him must worship him in spirit and in truth."[3] Then, in the first epistle of John, it reads: "My beloved, let us love one another; for love is from God; and everyone who loves is born of God and knows God. He who does not love, does not know God: For God is love."[4]

Therefore when we speak of "God" and "God's kingdom," we mean the power and presence of love unpretentiously moving in the hearts and minds of men, women and children all over the world. God's nature is pure spirit and love. This is God's covert kingdom at work!

The Pearl of Great Price

The following parable is one with which many are familiar. Some refer to it as the narrative of the Costly Pearl. When we carefully analyze the story, we discover a strange twist to this short parable. Jesus compares the kingdom to a merchant seeking pearls.

---

[3]Jn. 4:24, Aramaic Peshitta text.

[4]1 Jn. 4:7-8, Aramaic Peshitta text.

The Elusive Kingdom

*Heaven's sovereignty is like
a merchant who is searching for
precious pearls.
Then when he found an expensive pearl,
he went and sold all that he had
and purchased it.*[5]

Near Eastern Custom

We need to understand ancient Near Eastern customs to fully appreciate this simple, direct parable. Pearls, diamonds, and precious stones were not easily acquired in the Near East. In that entire period of antiquity, pearls were highly prized. People went diving in the Red Sea, the Persian Gulf, and the Indian Ocean searching for pearls. They used pearls for adornments, especially as necklaces. It is said that Cleopatra owned a pearl worth more than three million dollars.

In the Near East, merchants do not sell and purchase precious pearls in an open market. In our country, we display our costly stones and gems in windows of shops and inside glass counters of stores. In the ancient world, Near Easterners buried their precious gems and stones in the ground.

When a trader wished to purchase a gem, he had to search for it. It was not an easy task. People traded precious jewels secretly. Thus, when a merchant found a pearl, he would rush to sell some of his land so that he may purchase the precious gem before others discovered that the jewel was for sale.

---

[5]Mt. 13:45-46, Aramaic Peshitta text.

In Jesus' parable the trader sells **everything** that he has for the pearl. This leaves the merchant without any real property except for the pearl. What an ironic twist! He was so eager to obtain the precious pearl that he had to sell all that he possessed.

However, the merchant could have sold the pearl and earned even more than he had before. But, then, he would no longer possess the precious pearl that he had so diligently sought. Be that as it may, Jesus simply ended the story with the purchase of the pearl after the merchant sold all his possessions. As one can easily see, the pearl represented something more valuable to the merchant than all his original capital.

An Interpretation

God's kingdom, with its power and presence, is like a precious pearl. And because of its great value the kingdom becomes a challenge for everyone. First, you must search for it because it is not easy to find. Second, once you find it, you must sell everything to obtain it. After completing these requirements the pearl is yours. So what does this parable teach us?

The parable teaches us that after we find the presence of God (God's kingdom), and sell everything for it, in the end it really possesses us. Ultimately, we can experience God's kingdom, but in reality we can never possess, control, or manipulate it. No organization, priest, minister, religious or nonreligious officials, political power, or any individual is able to possess this kingdom. No one has exclusive rights (owner-ship) to heaven's sovereignty. This is the elusive kingdom of God.

The Most Famous Parable

Of all the stories that Jesus told, the most famous is the parable that Bible translators have named "The Prodigal Son." As I mentioned earlier in the book, Jesus never titled any of his parables. And many New Testament scholars believe that Jesus never interpreted his narratives. Nevertheless, we find that the synoptic gospels (Matthew, Mark, Luke) record Jesus interpreting some of his own stories. Some scholars suggest that the gospel writers or scribes placed these interpretations on Jesus' lips. Their purpose was to interpret Jesus' parables to meet the growing needs of the new Christian communities. Jesus' purpose was to proclaim God's kingdom to everyone.

Jesus' parables are extremely important. They reveal his discernment of God's activity in a world that did not recognize how God presences itself with, among, and through humanity. It was Jesus' vision of God. He understood that God always involves itself with humanity but not in the usual ways we often think. Jesus' parables are meant to change our thinking and perception of God—that is, the kingdom. We learn about God's nature, ways and dealings with the human family.

The parable of "the prodigal son" evolves around a father and his two boys. It tells us about the father's nature, and how this father responds to both his boys and not just to the prodigal. Realizing this, I have renamed the parable.

This is a tale about family relationships couched in an ancient, Semitic, Near Eastern pattern. Jesus weaves his moving and dramatic story around a specific family idea, mainly parental guidance and love. The psychology of a Semitic Eastern family is different from the West. (Jesus usually has God's kingdom in mind.)

The moment Jesus began his story with "A man had two

sons," his listeners knew there was a problem. There might be sibling rivalry or antagonism between the brothers. The Hebrew Bible contains many stories of friction between brothers—the narratives of Cain and Abel, Ishmael and Isaac, Jacob and Esau, Joseph and his brothers, and many others. Let us now begin the parable.

When Papa Acts like Mama

A man had two sons.
Now his younger son said to him:
My father give me the portion
that is coming to me from your house.
So he divided between them his property.

And after some days,
his younger son quickly collected
everything that was his share
and went into a far country,
and there he squandered his substance
living lavishly.

Now after he had spent everything,
there happened a great famine in that country,
and he began to lack.
So he went and connected
with one of the citizens of that country,
and he sent him to his field to feed hogs.
Now he was longing to feed his belly
from the carob beans that the hogs were eating,
but no one was giving to him.

And when he came to himself, he said:

How many hired hands are now in my father's house
abounding in bread
and here I am perishing from the famine.
I will get up and go to my father
and tell him:
My father, I sinned
against heaven and before you.
I no longer deserve to be called your son,
make me as one of your hired hands.
Then he got up and went to his father.

And while he still was at a distance,
his father saw him
and felt compassion for him.
So he ran
and fell upon his neck
and kissed him.

Then his son said to him:
My father,
I sinned against heaven and before you,
I do not deserve to be called your son.

But his father said to his servants:
Bring out the best robe and clothe him,
and put a ring on his finger, supply him with shoes.
Bring out the fat ox, and let us eat and be festive.
Because this my son was dead but is alive.
He was lost but is found.
So they began to be festive.

But there was his son, the elder one,
who was out in the field.

Now as he was coming,
he came up close to the house,
he heard the sound of many singing.
He called to one of the boys and asked him:
What is this?
He said to him: Your brother has come,
and your father has killed the fat ox, because
he got him back in good health.

Now he was furious
so he was not wanting to go in.
Then his father came out and pleaded with him.
But he said to his father:
See, how many years
I have slaved for you,
and never went against your orders.
Yet you never gave me even a goat
that I might throw a party with my friends.
But this son of yours
after he had squandered your wealth with harlots,
then came home, you killed the fat ox.

His father said to him:
My son, you are always with me,
and everything that is mine is yours.
It was necessary for us to be festive and joyful
because this brother of yours
was dead but is alive;
and was lost but is found![6]

---

[6]Lk.15:11-32, Aramaic Peshitta text.

The Commentary

Jesus begins his story saying: "A man had two sons. Now his younger son said to him: My father, give me the portion that is coming to me from your house. So he divided between them his property." No doubt, Jesus' audience responded with surprise and amazement as he began telling his tale.

Again, we need to look at Semitic, Near Eastern customs so that we may understand the background of Jesus' narrative. Usually an Eastern father centers his attention on the firstborn son. After all, he is the heir and successor. This special relationship between the father and the firstborn boy can and often does create problems with the younger son or sons in the family. Jealousy, disputes, and antagonism can arise between the oldest and the youngest. The older brother has complete authority over his mother, younger brothers, and sisters. He can buy and sell, receive guests, hire and fire laborers, and see after his father's servants.

According to Jesus' parable, the younger son asks for his inheritance right away. His father acquiesces to his son's wishes and divides the inheritance between his two boys. This was a foolish act. The townsfolk would have considered the father as unwise and overindulgent. In small towns news like this travels from home to home.

Jesus continues: "And after some days, his younger son quickly collected everything that was his share and went into a far country, and there he squandered his fortune living lavishly. Now after he had spent everything, there happened a great famine in that country, and he began to be in need. So he went to work for one of the citizens of that country, who sent him to his field to feed hogs. And he was longing to feed his belly from the carob beans that the hogs were eating."

Jesus began to draw sympathy from his listeners. They felt sorry for this pathetic young man. He was starving, broke, and had to do something which was unthinkable for an Israelite. He had to feed hogs. The Talmud says "Cursed be the man who would breed swine." This young Israelite is helping in their breeding. This part of the story is offensive and shameful!

Probably, Jesus' listeners are wondering what will happen to the young prodigal. The destitute boy had spent his entire inheritance. And now, starving and working for a Gentile, tending and feeding hogs, he couldn't even take enough action to put a carob bean in his mouth. Jesus hints at how spoiled this rich young man was. He was used to being served. After all, he belonged to a wealthy family.

There is something more to consider in this part of the narrative: "And he was longing to feed his belly from the carob beans. . ." A rabbinic maxim says: "Israel needs carobs to be forced to *tishuva* (repentance); that is, turn to God." This means that any person who has to eat carob beans is in abject poverty. And usually when an individual hits rock bottom, that person will turn (repent) and find his or her way up and out of the predicament. Turning to God is the way out for that person, according to rabbinic teaching.

"And when he [the prodigal] came to himself, he said: How many hired hands are now in my father's house abounding in bread and here I am perishing from the famine. I will get up and go to my father and tell him: My father, I sinned against heaven [a euphemism for "God"] and before you. I no longer deserve to be called your son, make me as one of your hired hands. Then, he got up and went to his father. And while he was still at a distance, his father saw him and felt compassion for him, so he ran and fell upon his neck and kissed him."

The erring son immediately tells his father that he had

sinned against God and before him. His father pays no attention to his repentance. He knows his son means what he says. He doesn't reprimand him and tell him, "I hope you've learned your lesson" or any other kind of scolding. His response was: "Bring out the best robe and clothe him, and put a ring on his hand, and supply him with shoes. And bring out and slay the fat ox, and let us throw a party. My son was dead but is alive. He was lost but is found. And so they threw a grand party."

The boy's father knows the pain and sorrow that are in his son's heart. He calls for the finest robe and family ring. His son is now fully reinstated. When the fat ox is slain, it means the boy receives great honor. The son's adornment and the feasting and music let the townsfolk know about his son's full restoration. But a dark cloud is about to blanket this joyful atmosphere. This ends part one of the story. For, you see, the narrative has more to tell us. It is not only about the prodigal son.

This story is in two acts. Act one is about the younger son, who squandered his inheritance living a wild and degenerate lifestyle. Act two will now move us in the direction of the older son. It will now center around a father and his two sons and not just the prodigal.

Part Two

The father had thrown a grand party for his youngest boy. He killed the fat ox; musicians and entertainers were present; the celebration was in full swing. Jesus introduces a new tension in the story. "But as the older son was coming from the field and drew close to the house, he heard the voices of many singing. He called to one of the boys and asked him: What is this?"

Once the older brother found out what was going on, he

became furious. Why should he enter the house and join the festivity? So, he didn't. His refusal to participate in the celebration was a slap in the face of both his parents. For now the older boy was shaming the household with his behavior. Not only this but he was also breaking the fourth commandment. He dishonored his father and mother. He shamed his father and brother publicly by not entering the house and partying with the others. Another reason for the anger was that he would now have to share what property was left with his younger brother. The older brother had right of possession but not disposition as long as the father was alive.

His father began pleading with his older son to join the festivities. Jesus continues: "But he said to his father: See how many years I have slaved for you and I never went against your orders! Yet, you never gave me even a goat so that I might throw a party with my friends. But after this son of yours had depleted your wealth with harlots and came home, you killed the fat ox!"

The older son complains about his dependency on his father and how slavish he had been as a worker. In his mind, he was the abused one. He also reminds his father that the younger brother had violated the family bloodline by joining himself to harlots. Family tension was at an all-time high. Jealousy, envy, and resentment were predominant at this celebration. How would the father resolve the tension? How does this parable relate to God's kingdom?

The Startling Ending

We have now reached the climax of Jesus' parable. The father of the two sons must answer the angry and resentful remarks of his oldest boy. In the closing lines of Jesus' story, the father responded to the indignation of his oldest son by saying: "My son, you are always with me! Everything that is mine is yours! It was necessary for us to throw a party and celebrate because your brother was dead and is alive. He was lost but is found!"

"My son you are always with me," means you are my constant companion. "Everything that is mine is yours," means you are co-owner of all I possess. What the older boy did not realize is that he made himself a slave in his father's house. For we need to see that he was slaving for something that already belonged to him. The celebration was his party, too!

As a stern, strict patriarch, this Near Eastern father was a failure. But he was a success at being a forgiving, nourishing mother. He had the physiology of a male but the soul and heart of a mother. This father loved both his sons and desired family unity and solidarity. Yes, he did spoil his children and brought some of the problems on the household. But in the end he was able to resolve it all.

God's kingdom (sovereign counsel and presence) doesn't divide the human family, but unifies! Infinite Intelligence or Divine Mind—whatever we wish to call God—is a loving presence that forgives, unifies, and works harmoniously with all humanity. God is no respecter of persons. God truly loves freely.

We set up rules and regulations that often divide the human race. One race may consider itself greater (older brother) than another; one religious group may believe itself superior to other sects; another group may think itself more righteous, holy, and pure than another. We draw lines of separation between sinner and saint, good and bad, but Jesus made it very clear about the love of God. We are all God's children.

Jesus taught that God as a father lets his sun shine upon the good and upon the bad, and lets his rain fall upon the just and the unjust. Jesus encouraged his disciples to be like their heavenly father. His story illustrates how the father refused to lose either son, both the good (older) boy and the prodigal. The father's loving kindness was sufficient for both sons, as God's grace is for all humanity.

A Strange Parable

In the gospel of Luke, we find an unusual short story. There is no explanation or interpretation in the text that follows this parable. Its placement in Luke's gospel is rather odd, also.

What More Can One Do?

A man had a fig tree
which was planted in his vineyard.
So he came looking for fruit from it.
But he did not find any.
Then, he told his worker: Look here,
for three years I have been coming,
wanting fruits on this fig tree,
but I never find any. Cut it down!
Why should it burden the ground?

The worker said to him:
My lord, let it alone this year also,
until I will dig around it
and manure it [literally: throw dung]
so it might bear fruits; if not,
then, you can cut it down.

An Interpretation

The owner was frustrated with his barren fig tree and wondered why it should burden the ground. Until the twentieth century, people in the Near East did not prize trees for shade or aesthetic beauty. They usually cut them down and burned them for fuel. If a fruit tree was dying or did not produce edible fruit, the owner would replace it.

Near Easterners plant fruit trees and depend on them for their living. Palestinians valued fruit trees very highly. The fig tree, an important food source, was one of the principal trees in ancient Palestine. Biblical writers used the fig tree as a metaphor to describe Israel's spiritual state. Among the Israelites, a flourishing fig tree was a blessing and a barren fig tree was a curse.

We may think of God's kingdom as one of fruitfulness and plenty, where things will just happen like magic, but Jesus changed this notion. An interpretation behind this story is that one had to keep working with principles of the kingdom. Prosperity and fruitfulness do not come overnight for everyone. Some are like the barren fig tree in this man's vineyard. We must keep on until our nurturing bears fruit. Spiritual principles work if we work them.

9

The Messianic Torah

It was a bright spring day in Northern Palestine when Jesus arrived by boat from the village of Capernaum. The gray waters of the lake of Galilee had been exceptionally calm and the air was filled with the sweet fragrance of the freshly blooming flowers in the nearby fields and mountainsides.

The boat had just reached the docking area near the town of Tiberias where a large number of the inhabitants had already started to gather by the seaside. When the news spread that Jesus and his disciples were in Tiberias, the narrow roads became crowded with multitudes of people bringing the sick and the suffering. Among the many pilgrims who came to hear the Nazarene were religious leaders, dissidents, and troublemakers. Some of them were ready to pledge their fidelity to the new *malpana* (teacher) while others had come only to challenge the provincial rabbi.

The Blessings

Upon seeing the crowds increasing in size, Jesus left the area and went up into the mountain. As he sat down, his disciples began to gather around him. The tall, dark, Near Eastern teacher sat silently with his right hand placed over his mouth looking deeply into the eyes of those who encircled him. For almost four hundred years no great prophet had arisen in Israel and the people were eager to hear what he had to say. Then Jesus broke his concentration, removed his hand from his mouth, and raised his eyes toward the clear Galilean sky. Glancing back to his disciples, he said in Aramaic: "*Toowayhon lmeskaynay brookh: dilhon hee malkutha dashmaya*," "Delighted are those who surrender to God because heaven's sovereign counsel belongs to them."[1]

The Humble

As Jesus uttered this first blessing, he had been pointing toward the gentle, humble, poor men and women in the crowd. Those who participate in this heavenly kingdom (God's sovereign presence) were not proud and arrogant but were unassuming and gentle in spirit. But who are those who surrender to God? They are those who transcend all racial, religious, national, cultural, and ancestral barriers leaving human pride, glory, and worldly honors completely behind them.

A Translation Difference

This verse usually translates as, "Blessed are the poor in spirit for theirs is the kingdom of heaven." Interestingly, most translators render the first beatitude literally from the Aramaic in all Greek and English versions of the gospel of Matthew. The Semitic phrase *lmeskaynay brookh* (literally, "poor in spirit") is a common Aramaic phrase referring to the poor who surrender everything, including themselves, to God. This Aramaic idiom refers to those who let God guide them. It refers to those who rely totally on God and not upon material things. God is always

---

[1]Mt. 5:3, Aramaic Peshitta text.

faithful, but material things come and go. In other words, God is "top priority" in their lives. According to rabbinic sources, in Judaism of the last two centuries B.C.E., the term "poor" had practically become a synonym for "pious" or "saintly." Matthew's rendering of Jesus saying "poor in spirit" has a specialized meaning and not just in the sense of those who possess nothing. Luke renders it "Delighted are the poor. . ."

Kingdom of Heaven

Again, in Matthew we have a specialized use of this term "kingdom of heaven." It means "God's kingdom." "Heaven" is a euphemistic term referring to "God." So the term "kingdom of heaven" signifies "God's sovereign presence." This kingdom is to affirm the powerful presence of heaven (God) in the hearts and souls of the peoples of the world. It symbolizes the universal establishment of justice, peace, love, joy, harmony, and goodness in the consciousness of every individual—a kingdom that is free of all greed, pride, and prejudice.

This kingdom has no boundaries or lines of division and separation. All kingdoms (nations) on earth have territorial limits. But this domain has no limits. It rules through spiritual principles. These principles are the spiritual laws of the universal Christ that guide the people who live in this heavenly awareness.

The Meaning of "Blessed"

The Aramaic term *toowayhon*, "blessed," comes from the root *toov,* implying something "good." *Toowayhon* means "happy, content, blissful, delighted, fortunate." Some translators use the words "lucky" or "fortunate." Still, these translations do not carry the full impact of this Semitic word. It means the best that a place or person has. This also means "good" in every variety and sense of the word "good" such as "well-being," "beauty," "success," and "joy."

The Mourners

"*Toowayhon laweelay: dhenon nethbayun.*" "Delighted are the wailing ones, for they will be consoled!"[2] Those who wail refers to those who were suffering injustices, who were mourning the seemingly delayed coming of God's presence, those who longed for God's order, peace, and goodness.

Throughout many generations in Israel, the prophets referred to a small group of faithful people whom they called "the remnant." These people had been aware of the real nature and power of God's kingdom, aware that the heavenly treasures it offered were actually living spiritual principles and truths that could transform the hearts of people, eliminating injustice and violence.

But when would this kingdom appear? When would God right the wrongs of humanity? Jesus directed his comforting words and blessings to these mourners, assuring them that the time for solace was at hand. They were now to realize that the kingdom of heaven was within their reach. They were soon to participate as citizens of the new kingdom of joy and gladness.

No doubt, these mourners quickly recalled the prophetic words of their great statesman and prophet Isaiah when he said:

---

[2]Mt. 5:4, Aramaic Peshitta text.

"The spirit of the Lord is upon me, because the Lord has anointed [appointed] me and sent me to declare the joyful message to the meek; to bind up the broken hearted, to proclaim liberty to captives, and release to prisoners; to proclaim the acceptable year of the Lord, and the day of salvation of our God. **To comfort all those who mourn; to give to the mourners of Zion beauty instead of ashes, perfume instead of mourning, a cloak of beauty instead of the spirit of heaviness**; they shall be called men of justice, the planting of the Lord which is glorious."[3] The mourners to whom Jesus addressed this blessing understood that the predicted time of fulfillment was now upon them.

The Meek

"*Toowayhon lmakeyhey: dhenon nertoon araa.*" "Delighted are the meek, for they will inherit the land."[4] Some scholars believe that this beatitude originally followed the first blessing as an explanation of Jesus' saying. In other words, Jesus didn't really utter this beatitude. Be that as it may, it is still a practical teaching even if it is Semitic conventional wisdom. The biblical psalmist of old sang "the meek will inherit the land and will delight themselves in the abundance of peace."[5] Again, the prophet Zephaniah declared: "Seek the Lord, all you meek of the earth, execute justice; seek justice and meekness. . ."[6]

---

[3]Isa. 61:1-3, Aramaic Peshitta text.

[4]Mt. 5:5, Aramaic Peshitta text.

[5]Ps. 37:11, Aramaic Peshitta text.

[6]Zeph. 2:3, Aramaic Peshitta text.

Meekness is a quality of God's presence in humanity which all too often lies dormant. To awaken this latent force and encourage its growth, this beatitude blesses meekness within every person. The meek or humble are those who are yielding, pliable, flexible, and unassuming. They are free of anger that often initiates disputes and violence. Landowners in the ancient Near East, for example, preferred to lease their farms and vineyards to the meek because they were reliable and not troublemakers. Also when a man dies or is killed in battle, leaving no male heir, the deserving meek will usually obtain his property.

Meekness of attitude, mind, and heart helps us to live more freely and happily in this world. Trees that bend in a storm will survive the storm. When we roll with the punches, we will live more abundantly. Arthritic thinking (unbending thoughts) only stiffens our attitudes and makes it harder for us to live well.

Before Jesus uttered another blessing, a contemplative mood settled over him, and a restful quiet seemed to envelop the entire group. For a few moments it appeared as if the Master-Teacher was seeing a vision. Perhaps Jesus might have been contemplating how long Israel had struggled for freedom. After all, his nation had fought with the Egyptians, Assyrians, Syrians, Chaldeans, and the Greeks—and now their conflict was with Rome. It seemed that not only Israel's history, but also all nations' histories, testified to the human battle with hatred, revenge, subjugation, and violence. Was there an answer? Jesus breached the silence: *"Toowayhon laylain dkapneen wazhain lkaynootha: dhenon nesbayun."*

"Delighted are those who hunger and thirst for justice, for they will be full."[7] These words of Jesus shattered the silence

---

[7]Mt. 5:6, Aramaic Peshitta text.

and ignited the hearts of his followers. He taught that only as one deeply hungers and thirsts for true piety (justice and goodness) will one see godliness. A genuine godliness is divine justice.

All imperial powers that have had double standards in their policies have destroyed themselves. Injustice sooner or later exacts its toll from all those who practice it. Israel, throughout biblical history, has seen the rise and fall of many great imperial nations. Yet the Israelites had refused to receive guidance from their prophets. They had failed to accept the admonition of their great prophet-statesmen, and to work in the interest of God's kingdom.

Jesus' saying may be paraphrased as: "Delighted are those of you who are seeking goodness not only for your own nation but are hungry and thirsty for the reign of godly justice and truth for all nations!" True justice must begin in the hearts and minds of people everywhere before any nation can fully demonstrate "justice for all." The power of justice lies not in legislation alone, but in the movement of love radiating from enlightened hearts. This beatitude inspired a profound response in the men and women who heard it.

The Compassionate

It was late afternoon. The day had been hot, but cool dry air now began to sweep across the lake of Galilee, refreshing the eager multitudes who had come to hear Jesus teach on the mountainside. The Master stood up, focused his attention, and said: *"Toowayhon lamrahmanay: dalayhon nehoon rahmay."* "Delighted are the compassionate for they will receive compassion."[8]

His audience understood this because Easterners are usually very giving and extremely hospitable, not only to their neighbors, but also to strangers and even to their enemies. Near Easterners often say: "Today we have plenty but no one knows what tomorrow will bring. The same hand that renders help today may be in need of assistance tomorrow. No one can live to himself." This is a spiritual principle: To those who are compassionate, compassion will come to them also; to those who are loving, love will return to them; and those who are giving will never lack. Although people appear as separate beings, they are truly one with all life, which is indivisible. Therefore, actions of mercy and kindness return to the doer.

Again, many New Testament scholars think that Jesus did not utter this beatitude, but it speaks of the conventional wisdom of the time. However, whether Jesus said this or not, the principle still holds true. We are distinguished by our deeds of mercy and compassion, and not just by our words of mercy alone. Charitable and loving acts that spring from a compassionate heart are actions of God flowing from human beings. All nature is founded on the principle of giving and receiving. This pattern was established by our wise God and when this balance is disturbed, all life is disturbed.

Pure in Heart

Jesus now glanced toward another group of followers and said: *"Toowayhon laylain dadkain blibhon denon nehzon*

---

[8]Mt. 5:7, Aramaic Peshitta text.

lalaha."[9] "Delighted are those who are pure in their hearts for they will see God." Biblical scholars deem this beatitude and the one that follows as a scribal or Matthean insertion rather than the voice of Jesus. For me, the teaching is still valid even if it is an insertion. "Pure in heart" in Aramaic means "those who are clear in their minds and hearts." Only a mind that is clear can transcend its own personal wants and gratifications and see God. It also refers to anyone who is "sincere." God is pure love and goodness; pure love has no object or subject but is simply loving, whereas personal hatred, resentments, and vindictiveness cloud the heart from seeing Reality—God. "To the pure all things are pure." Humanity must see (perceive) God so that it might understand its own true nature, for humanity is the image and likeness of God. We might add— when we are as pure light we may shine upon those who are groping in the dark for understanding. And through a clear mind we can see others and discern our real self in them.

The humble, the mourners, the meek, those who suffered for the sake of justice, the merciful, and the pure in heart were to be exemplary citizens of the heavenly kingdom that was to reign upon the earth. These people were to be the perfect cornerstones for the foundation of a new world order. They were to be free of all materialism so that they might be a lamp to the feet of others and a light on the pathway of life. These are not superior beings but they are forerunners of the manifestation of God's active, loving presence in the world.

---

[9]Mt. 5:8, Aramaic Peshitta text.

The Peacemakers

The crowds near Jesus sat silently as the sun slowly disappeared behind the lofty Galilean hills. Among the throngs of people, who had come to listen or to be healed by the provincial teacher of Nazareth, were the peacemakers. These newcomers had worked their way through the multitudes to draw nearer to the Master-Teacher.

Jesus' apostles standing next to him saw the peacemakers approaching and immediately made room for them, seating them directly in front of their Master. The resonant, gentle voice of the prince of peace reached out and embraced those who were gathered so close to him as he said: "*Toowayhon lawday shlama davnow dalaha nethdron.*" "Delighted are the peacemakers for they are called God's children."[10]

In the Near East "peacemakers" were those who found peace within themselves and, therefore, had the ability to help solve the difficulties of other members of their community. These men usually sat outside the city gates and would act as judges, settling quarrels and disputes among the people. They received no remuneration for their services. The public trusted these men and they were often called "sons of God." Now, this saying made it very clear that peacemakers were citizens of the heavenly presence known as God's kingdom—a kingdom of peace, joy, and righteousness.

"Peace" in Aramaic is *shlama* and it means "to surrender." When Near Easterners greet each other they say: *Shlama lookh,* "peace to you." It means "hello" but literally means "I surrender to you." And when the salutation is returned, then the two become one and will protect each other.

---

[10]Mt. 5:9, Aramaic Peshitta text.

Thus, "peace" is a synonym for "God." Peacemakers are called God's children because they demonstrate the reign of harmony and tranquility. These peacemakers work in the interest of everyone —the rich and the poor, the strong and the weak, those of noble birth and those of humble birth. These children of God have transcended self-interest and spontaneously respond to the universal law of life.

When Jesus finished these blessings, the great teacher's words had stunned the crowds, for he taught them as one who had power and not as their own scribes and Pharisees. Jesus taught the kingdom principles to the simple, peasant people of Galilee; this was truly the messianic Torah. God's presence was active on earth through the people.

10

Perfection

In chapters five through seven in the gospel of Matthew, we have the collected teachings of Jesus that New Testament translators have named "The Sermon on the Mount." I refer to it as the "Messianic Torah." There is a recorded saying of Jesus in this gospel that appears to be an impossible command. "Be ye therefore perfect, even as your Father which is in heaven is perfect."[1] We might question how one can become perfect even as God is perfect? Why would Jesus command such perfection from his disciples? To understand what Jesus meant by his use of the word "perfect," we again need to turn to the Aramaic language.

The Meaning of Perfection

Most of us usually equate being "perfect" with total flawlessness and infallibility, but the Aramaic term does not imply any such notion. Many of us labor under the idea that we must be perfect. The Aramaic word *gmeera* does mean "perfect," but in the sense of "complete," "thorough," "finished," "full-grown," "mature," "accomplished," "comprehensive," "rounded out," and "all-inclusive." In the Near East when a young man arrives at full maturity, he is a *"gmeera"*— "a man of understanding." It also refers to anyone who is very thorough in whatever she or he does.

---

[1]Mt. 5:48, KJV.

Jesus' Intention

What Jesus desired of his disciples was a thorough comprehension of the task that was before them. Because they were to face much opposition and many clever people, they needed to be wise, alert, gentle, unaffected, and courageous. These disciples were not to be exclusive in their approach to others, but "all-inclusive." The notion of "insiders" versus "outsiders" was not to be a part of their understanding.

Before Jesus told his disciples to become perfect, he had taught them: "Love your enemies, bless anyone who curses you, do good to anyone who hates you, and pray for those who carry you away by force and persecute you, so that you may be sons of your Father who is in heaven, who causes the sun to shine upon the good and the bad, and who pours down his rain upon the just and the unjust."[2] This is the perfection to which Jesus referred. And just as God does not discriminate but is "all-inclusive," so his children were to show the same nonexclusive nature as their "heavenly Father."

Jesus makes no demands upon humans to be flawless or infallible. For who can say what perfection truly is? Perfection is based on comparison. Different cultures have various ideas about perfection. What may be perfect in one particular setting would not be in another. Besides, what may be perfect today may become imperfect tomorrow. Perfection is a loving presence. It is the loving presence that is all-inclusive. This loving presence knows no sex, race, color, creed, barriers, or boundaries. Each stage of human development is its own perfection. A loving presence is a presence where harmony, peace, and joy manifest in one's heart and mind. This is God in

---

[2]Mt. 5:44-45, Aramaic Peshitta text, Lamsa translation.

action. Jesus encouraged his disciples to accept and treat everyone in the same manner as God blesses the good and the bad, the just and the unjust.

11

Forgiveness

"Then Peter approached him and said to him: My lord, if my brother should wrong me, how many times should I forgive him? Up to seven times? Jesus said to him: I do not tell you up to seven times, but up to seventy times seven, seven times."[1] Why did Jesus tell Peter, "Up to seventy times seven, seven times?" This is typical Aramaic speech. It is the Semitic way of saying one needs to forgive "a limitless number of times." Most of us have a limit on forgiveness. Certain things are forgivable and others are not. Then how long should one keep forgiving the same thing? Jesus answered this question.

Of all the many good things Jesus taught, the two things he stressed the most were love and forgiveness. He definitely was an advocate of forgiveness. This is one of the basic teachings that makes his gospel so appealing and powerful to so many people. In his famous prayer known as the "Lord's Prayer," or the "Our Father," Jesus said: "And release (forgive) us from our offenses (cancel our debts) even as we have released our offenders (debtors)."[2] There exist many more sayings of Jesus that express the notion of forgiveness, but despite the great emphasis, a large number of people have a difficult time when confronting a challenging situation that calls for the practice of forgiveness.

---

[1]Mt. 18:21-22, Aramaic Peshitta text.

[2]Mt 6:12, Aramaic Peshitta text.

The Meaning of Forgiveness

What does "forgiveness" mean? How do we find the ability to forgive, especially when in the middle of a very trying circumstance? The Aramaic word *shwak* means "to forgive," "to remit," "to set free," "to cancel," "to release," and "to let go." But how do we "let go?" It is especially difficult when we feel like holding on and never forgiving? What is it that makes us hold on to a particular person or situation that needs to be released? We usually hang on to our anger because there is some interest involved.

As long as we feel and think that there will be a "payoff" or "dividend" for holding grudges and resentments, forgiveness becomes very difficult to practice. However, when we lose interest in something, we simply let it go. Where there is an emotional investment, the interest in retaliation is strong and it ties us to the problem. It is always good to remember that whatever we send out, emotionally or mentally, we always keep the original energy and notion that has imprinted itself on our brain cells. After all, we are the generator for our emotions and thoughts. Now there must be something more to consider that is beyond the momentary "payoff" or resentment.

Turning to God

The Psalmist says, "Turn to me and know that I am God."[3] It is in turning to God and coming to *know* God that we find the power to forgive, to let go of any person or situation. In reality, this is the key to resolving all difficult circumstances. However,

---

[3]Ps. 46:10, Aramaic Peshitta text.

we may still question the value of forgiveness. Or, we may wonder how we may acquire the motivation to become forgiving while in the middle of a very bad situation. Although we know that resentments and deep-seated anger may translate themselves into illness, often this does not seem to provide a strong enough incentive for us to practice forgiveness. Then, what will help us?

When our attention is **totally captivated by a loving, joyful emotional state**, then we have less interest in spending many days, or even hours, in emotional turmoil and upheaval. Turning to God and knowing God becomes paramount in our life. God is love, peace, and joy—and who does not want to be loving, peaceful, and joyful? We can begin to recognize our original, essential nature, which is love, peace, and joy. We begin to discover the divine energy of forgiveness. When we are deeply aware that we, of ourselves, are powerless, then we can know the power of the Spirit that abides in us. We move beyond our limited emotional state and discern the boundless energy of the human spirit that is divine. Zechariah, the prophet, declared: "Not by might, nor by power, but by my spirit, saith the Lord of hosts."[4]

The Healing Power of Forgiveness

Forgiveness is a powerful antidote to many faltering relationships, adverse conditions, and even to self-hatred. Forgiveness is compassion in action. A false, condescending act of forgiveness can become an arrogant act, but a sincere release of others and yourself demonstrates the vital power of love and compassion.

---

[4]Zech. 4:6, KJV.

The act of forgiveness comes from our spiritual self (our essential being) and expresses the presence of our heavenly Father and God's kingdom in our world. Again, let us consider the words of Jesus from his famous prayer: "And free us from our offenses even as we have freed our offenders."

12

Fasting and Prayer

"One from the crowd answered and said: Teacher, I brought my son to you, because he has a spirit of dumbness. And whenever it seizes him, it torments him; and he foams, and gnashes his teeth, and becomes tired out. And I asked your disciples to heal him but they could not. . .then Jesus rebuked the illness (unclean spirit). . .and the epileptic cried out much, and was tormented. Then the boy became as if dead, so that many could say: He is dead. Now Jesus took him by the hand and lifted him up. When Jesus entered the home his disciples asked him privately: Why could we not heal him? He said to them: This kind cannot be healed by anything except through fasting and prayer."[1]

Fasting

Dr. George M. Lamsa used to say that fasting was first instituted so the rich might have sympathy and understanding for the conditions of the poor. In the East when rich men fast, they are very generous in their gifts to the poor because during a time of fasting they have a taste of poverty and hunger. Fasting was also recommended for the sick in the Near East. They believed it gave the body time to rest so that it might cleanse and heal itself.

Moses, Elijah, and Jesus had fasted for forty days, not to

---

[1]Mk. 9:14-29, Aramaic Peshitta text.

heal their bodies but to clear their minds so that they might see and hear God's guidance. Fasting weakens the physical energies of the body but, at the same time, it increases the spiritual forces within the healer and helps him discern the true nature of wholeness.

Jesus evidently recommended fasting and prayer in the practice of healing. It seems that since certain illnesses appeared to be more difficult to heal than others, fasting and prayer would aid the healer in his work. As the above episode from the Bible indicates, the disciples could not heal the epileptic because their hearts and minds were not fully prepared to heal.[2]

Prayer

Prayer calms our fears and floods the mind with peace. It also deepens the awareness of our union with the source of our being—God. Through fasting and prayer the mind becomes a clear channel of pure spiritual consciousness—a confidence will permeate the healer and the ill individual. Healing energy, like electricity, needs a clear path, free of resistance, so it may be conducted properly. Fasting and prayer produce a peaceful, receptive mind that is free from all invalid concepts and thoughts. This is how the healer then becomes the agency through which the healing energy flows and expresses.

---

[2]See Errico &. Lamsa, *Aramaic Light on the Gospels of Mark and Luke,* "Fasting and Prayer," pp. 52-53.

13

Born of Spirit

"Jesus answered and said to him: What I say to you is absolutely true that if a person is not reborn, he cannot see God's kingdom. Nicodemus said to him: How can an old man be reborn? Is he able to enter his mother's womb a second time and be born? Jesus replied and said to him: What I say to you is absolutely true that if a person is not born of water and of spirit, he cannot enter God's kingdom. What is created by the body is another body; and what is created by the Spirit is spirit. Do not be surprised that I have told you that all of you must be reborn. The wind blows where it pleases and its sound you hear, but you do not know from where it comes or to where it goes; so it is with everyone who is born of the Spirit."[1]

Background

Jesus proclaimed the gospel of God's coming kingdom. Through his ministry of teaching, healing, and exorcism, God's presence (kingdom) manifested itself in word and power. The evidence is so weighty that even modern biblical scholars, who seem to disagree about almost everything else, are one-hundred percent in agreement that Jesus' message was God's kingdom. All three so-called synoptic gospels (Matthew, Mark, Luke) emphasize Jesus' gospel of the kingdom.

The episode before us is more than likely based on Jesus'

---

[1]Jn. 3:3-8, Aramaic Peshitta text.

sayings about the kingdom. However, the entire scene depicted in John 3:1-21 is mostly fictitious. It conveys some of the early ideas of the Christian Church about Jesus. This is so evident that when Jesus refers to water baptism in verse 5, "born of water," it prompted a conservative scholar to remark that "his whole expose would appear more natural on the lips of a Christian catechist long after the Church's foundation than on Jesus' lips."

Jesus and Nicodemus

Jesus speaks to Nicodemus in a typically Aramaic style of speech. The phrase *amen, amen, amar'a lhon*, "truly, truly, I say to you," is vividly and distinctively Aramaic. I translated the phrase as "What I say to you is absolutely true." When the Semitic word *amen* appears at the beginning of a sentence, it denotes truthfulness, faithfulness and something that is absolutely true. Also the idioms *mitheelid min dresh*, "born again" or "reborn," is a Northern Galilean Aramaic term of speech. It means "to become like a little child." Interestingly, in Aramaic the word for "little boy" is *yalda* and the word for "born" is *yalad*.

Jesus had told his disciples that unless they become like little children they would not enter God's kingdom. What we have in these verses is a parallel teaching of Jesus in harmony with the synoptic gospels. However, the phrase "born of water" puts a new twist on Jesus' teaching. The gospel writer makes water baptism a necessity to enter the kingdom.

John's Idea

John presents a new view on Jesus' thought about God's kingdom. He expands the idea of seeing and entering God's kingdom by being "born again." It is John who puts the Aramaic idiom "reborn" on the lips of Jesus. Since God is heavenly one must be born from above. For one to understand God's sovereignty, which is of the heavenly realms, one must have a corresponding heavenly nature to perceive what is from above. Thus, one must be "born again."

Nonetheless, Nicodemus did not grasp the meaning of this Northern Galilean idiom. He reasoned from a literal sense. Can he enter his mother's womb and be born a second time? The reply to Nicodemus was: "If a person is not born of water and of spirit he cannot enter God's kingdom." Water is symbolic of outward cleansing. Spirit is symbolic of inner cleansing. One must be totally transformed! For the gospel writer this expression "born of water and spirit" meant a brand-new beginning.

God's Kingdom

God's rule is not discerned with earthly eyes but only through a new spirit and insight. This kingdom is present on earth, but it is only a transformed human being who can perceie and enter into the activity of God's sovereignty. An alteration of one's heart and mind brings about the ability to see and participate in God's sovereign presence.

"What is created by a human body is another physical form, but what is created by the Spirit is spiritual. Don't be surprised because I have told you that everyone must be reborn." To make it very clear, the writer has Jesus explain that he is not speaking physically but spiritually. It is the Spirit that brings about this spiritual rebirth and it has nothing to do with human reproduction.

"The wind blows where it pleases and its sound you hear, but you do not know from where it comes or to where it goes; so it is with everyone who is born of the Spirit." This mysterious birth cannot be totally explained. It is an inward experience. How can one give a full explanation of this kind of transformation or rebirth? It is like the wind, which to the ancients was a mysterious force. God's spirit is like the wind. One cannot completely rationalize the workings of Spirit.

In those ancient days people did not understand the birth of the wind (from where it comes) nor what happens to it— that is, how it dies (to where it goes). The above scriptural passage cannot be speaking about the wind's direction. For even in those days, they understood about the direction of the wind, whether it was a southerly or westerly wind. The wind's source was a mystery to them. They did not know how it was formed and how it died. Thus, the mysterious birth of the Spirit is the same as the wind. It is strange and mysterious to those who only think of human birth. A heavenly nature rules those born of the spirit. "As you do not know the path of the wind, and the manner of a woman who is with child; even so you do not know the works of the Lord who makes all."

14

A Camel and a Needle's Eye

"And again I say to you, It is easier for a camel to go through the eye of a needle than for a rich man to enter into the kingdom of God."[1] Did Jesus teach that it is impossible for a rich man to enter God's kingdom? Let us now turn to the Aramaic text of the gospel of Matthew. "Again I say to you, It is easier for a rope to go through the eye of a needle, than for a rich man to enter into the kingdom of God."[2]

The Aramaic Meaning of *Gamla*

In Aramaic, the word *gamla* has three distinct meanings: "a camel," "a rope," and "a beam." The context will determine the proper English translation of *gamla*. In this passage of Matthew's gospel, Jesus' reference to "needle" clearly establishes that context. Interestingly, Eastern women often refer to a very thick thread as a "rope."

Among Aramaic-speaking people of the Near East, one might hear the populace talking about different degrees of friendship, especially when meeting new people. For instance, a Near Easterner may say: "When we met, it was like a thread passing through the eye of a needle." This means "We hit it off nicely" or "We got along just beautifully." In other words, there

---

[1]Mt. 19:24, KJV.

[2]Mt. 19:24, Aramaic Peshitta text, Lamsa translation.

were no hitches in the relationship.

Jesus, in this particular saying, taught that the wealthy must learn to share their riches so that they could participate in God's kingdom. However, he knew that it would not be easy for many of the rich to comply with this notion. Therefore, he used the term "rope" to suggest difficulty, and not "camel" which implies impossibility.

A Misunderstanding

Some Bible authorities claim that Jesus was not actually referring to a needle's eye but to a little gate or door in the wall that surrounded Near Eastern cities. Dr. Abraham M. Rihbany, a Near Easterner, in his book *The Syrian Christ* makes the following comment about this Western idea of a gate in the wall called "the needle's eye."

> The walled cities and feudal castles of Palestine, the explanation runs, have large gates. Because of their great size, such gates are opened only on special occasions to admit chariots and caravans. Therefore, in order to give pedestrians thoroughfare, a smaller opening about the size of an ordinary door is made in the center of the great gate, near to the ground. Now this smaller door through which a camel cannot pass is the "eye of the needle" mentioned in the Gospel. . . .However, the chief trouble with this explanation of the "eye of the needle" passage is that it is wholly untrue. This saying is current in the East, and in all probability it was a common saying there long before the advent of Christ. But I never knew that small door in a city or castle gate to be called the needle's eye; nor indeed the large gate to be called the needle. The name of that door, in

the common speech of the country, is called the *"plum,"* and I am certain the Scriptural passage makes no reference to it whatever.[3]

Jesus did not make it difficult for wealthy people to enter the kingdom. He simply taught that shared wealth brings a common joy to all and can meet the needs of many. There are also some interpreters who recognize this passage of Scripture as a hyperbole and do not take it literally. This idea is also typical of Semitic speech.

---

[3]Abraham Rihbany, *The Syrian Christ*, "Impressions vs. Accuracy," pp. 130-132.

15

Let the Dead Bury the Dead

There is a verse of scripture in the gospel of Matthew that has puzzled many Bible students and has raised doubts about Jesus' character. It has been difficult for many people to believe that Jesus would make such a cruel remark. This is what is recorded: "And another of his disciples said unto him, Lord suffer me first to go and bury my father; But Jesus said unto him, Follow me; and let the dead bury their dead."[1]

Idiomatic Expressions

Jesus understood exactly what the man meant when he said: "Suffer me first to go bury my father." "To bury one's father" is an Aramaic idiom and it means, "My father is an old man (one who is over seventy years of age). And I must support him until he passes away." In the Near East and especially in that area where Dr. George M. Lamsa was born, the people consider a man who reaches the age of seventy as dead. In other words, he has finished his work and appears to have no more interest in life. They believe he can no longer be productive nor does he have any earning power. He will then entrust everything to his oldest son.

A man passed the age of seventy expects his children to care for him. One often hears Near Easterners say: "My father is dead and is put in his coffin and the coffin is waiting beside

---

[1]Mt. 8:21-22, KJV.

114

the grave to be lowered." But this saying really means: "My father may die any day. He is very old and may go quickly."

However, we still have a problem with Jesus' saying ,"Let the dead bury the dead." Dr. Lamsa suggests the probability that Jesus actually said: "Let the town bury the dead" or "let the community take care of the older people." The reason for this suggestion is that Dr. Lamsa believes a copying error occurred in the manuscript. He says that the Aramaic word for dead is *metta* and the word for town is *matta.* The difference in the formation of the words and the pronunciation is slight and was therefore a copyist's error.

He also says that if a tiny dot under the second letter of the Aramaic word for dead is missing, the copyist might easily be misled. These dots, or vowel points, were not known when the gospel was first written. He also suggests that old manuscripts were often blurred and mutilated. And his final conclusion was that it would have sounded harsh for Jesus to have made such an insensitive remark.[2]

The man's father was not dead at the time that he was listening to Jesus. Had this been the case, he would have been busy burying his father, for Semites bury their dead soon after they die.

There is one other idea we may consider about this troublesome verse. Among the Assyrian-Chaldean people today, there is an idiom still in use: *Shwoq meetheh dqry meethay.* It is the same idiomatic expression as in Matthew 8:22, "Let the dead bury their dead." But the meaning of this idiom today is, "Don't become involved in other people's problems. Let them take care of their own difficulties." The Assyrians and Chaldeans of today usually give this advice to those people who do not mind their

---

[2]See Errico & Lamsa, *Aramaic Light on the Gospel of Matthew,* "Burying One's Father," pp. 129-130.

own business. Jesus could also be saying: "Let others take care of their own problems. You follow me." There are many suggested interpretations of this difficult verse but Dr. Lamsa's interpretation seems to be the most appealing explanation.

16

An Ordinary Human Being

"But Jesus was silent. Then the High Priest said to him: I command you by the living God that you tell us if you are the Messiah (Anointed), the son of God? Jesus answered him: You have said that! But I say to you that from now on you will see this human being sitting on the right hand of power and coming on the clouds of the sky!"[1]

The High Priest had been questioning Jesus to see if he could convict him of blasphemy. He had heard that this Galilean peasant had been assuming the noble title of Messiah and also had been referring to himself as God's son. No one but a descendant of the royal house of David would dare to assume these titles. But the High Priest had misunderstood the sonship of Jesus and interpreted it in a physical sense.

Jesus kept silent before this high ecclesiastical figure. However, when the Priest charged him to speak, he had to respond. Jesus' reply, "You have said that," meant "You misinterpret my teaching about divine sonship. It is spiritual, not physical." But Jesus continued to tell not only the High Priest but the entire assembly of priests, "From now on you will see this human being sitting on the right hand of power and coming on the clouds of glory." There are several Aramaic expressions in Jesus' reply that need clarification—"right hand of power," "clouds of glory," and the term "human being."

---

[1]Mt. 26:63-64, Aramaic Peshitta text.

The Son of Man

An Aramaic expression that still continues to vex New Testament scholars is the term *bar-nasha*. It literally translates as "The Son of Man," but it means a "human being," an "ordinary man." Jesus almost always used this Aramaic expression *bar-nasha* when referring to himself. He very seldom, if at all. used the term *bar dalaha*, "son of God."

"The son of man" is strictly Semitic terminology. Scholars term this expression when translated into Greek as a "literary monstrosity. In Hellenistic or classical Greek it would translate as "the son of the man" or simply "the man's son." This rendering is totally inappropriate and inadequate.

Jesus' Rejection of Titles

Israel, as a nation, expected a militant and political Messiah. He was to come from the royal lineage of David and therefore have the right to rule in the messianic kingdom. Jesus, instead of assuming this earthly title, more frequently claimed to be an "ordinary human being." It was his way of answering those who constantly argued about his ancestry and nobility. Jesus was no pretender to any earthly throne. His leadership as the Messiah represented a spiritual kingdom of God's presence that was to reside in the hearts and souls of the peoples of all nations.

In Semitic thought, the qualities of God are often described in human terms. "Sitting on the right hand of God or power" is a figurative expression that signifies "total power and authority." As a general rule, the queen has the seat at the king's right hand. When the queen is absent, this place is occupied by the princes and noblemen of the realm as a token of appreciation and great

118

honor.

"Clouds of the sky" is another Aramaic expression that means "great glory and honor" and "the highest achievement and success." Jesus was to be successful although the High Priest had intended to put an end to his earthly life.

A paraphrased translation from the Aramaic text of this verse would read: "Jesus said to him, You have said that! But I say to you that from now on you will see this ordinary person with total power and authority achieving the highest honor." In a matter of four or five generations the power and truth of Jesus as Messiah spread throughout the world with tremendous authority. His teaching shook the world! Kings and emperors of the East and West were frightened by the powerful energy and force that carried these teachings. Jesus' power and presence as a spiritual Messiah and his kingdom were felt everywhere.

17

The Transfiguration

"Jesus took Simon, Jacob, and John and went up into a mountain to pray. And while he prayed, the appearance of his face was changed and his clothes became white and dazzling. And behold two men were speaking with him who were Moses and Elijah. . . .And when they began to leave him, Simon said to Jesus: Teacher, it is better for us to remain here. . . .And when he had said these things, there came a cloud, saying: This is my son, the beloved, hear him. And when the voice was heard, they found Jesus alone."[1] "And as they were coming down from the mountain, Jesus commanded them, and said to them: Do not speak of this vision in the presence of anyone. . ."[2]

Many New Testament scholars believe that the transfiguration experience was originally a vision that the Apostle Simon (Peter) received after Jesus' resurrection had occurred. They also suggest that when it was recorded it was placed in the gospels as a pre-Easter event. This may be so. Nonetheless, I have confined my comments to the placement of this episode as it appears in Matthew and Luke as a pre-Easter happening. So I will not be commenting on the transfiguration as a post-Easter event, although this notion may be true.

Jesus' transfiguration was a spiritual event. Matthew in his gospel records the event as a vision. The disciples of Jesus had anticipated ruling and reigning with him and sitting upon actual

---

[1]Lk. 9:28-36, Aramaic Peshitta text.

[2]Mt. 17:9, Aramaic Peshitta text.

physical thrones. They had expected to govern the twelve tribes of Israel and, eventually, the world. His disciples had no idea that Jesus' mission was to inaugurate a spiritual kingdom.

They also believed, as many in their nation also did, that Moses and Elijah would return from heaven in their original bodily forms. This event was the first slight realization in the three apostles' minds that their Master's mission represented a spiritual reality. Now they saw that Moses and Elijah had returned spiritually. Moses, as a symbol, represented the idea that Jesus' teaching was the fulfillment of the *Torah*. Elijah's appearance also represented the notion that Jesus was the fulfillment of the prophets.

The transfiguration was only a small beginning in the consciousness of Peter, Jacob (James), and John. At this time these three apostles recognized Jesus' divine nature. Eventually, through the resurrection and ascension of Jesus, all the apostles came to realize Jesus' spiritual-divine nature. It is through the revelation of Jesus' divinity that humanity becomes aware of its own spiritual origin. Thus, the transfiguration is also the revelation of humanity's divine sonship through Christ.

18

The Second Coming of Christ

When will Jesus return to the earth? Will he return in a physical body? Will the events be as terrible and frightful as we have been told? What true significance, if any, is there to the second coming of Christ? These are just a few of the questions I am often asked about the return of Christ.

The subject of biblical prophecy, especially about the second coming of the Christ, is so enormous it would take a detailed and special volume to reply to this theme. My intention in this brief chapter is only to touch on a few salient points and to clarify some areas of the so-called "Second Coming."

Again, many New Testament scholars believe that Jesus did not teach an apocalyptic eschatology.[1] And they do not believe that Jesus will return with an army from heaven to bring violence and vengeance on a disbelieving humanity. These scholars suggest that the writers (scribes) added these notions when they wrote the apocalyptic 24th chapter of Matthew. In other words, these words were put on the lips of Jesus. This may be so. But I am directing my comments to the Aramaic idiomatic expression and style of speech recorded in the 24th chapter of Matthew.

---

[1]Eschatology comes from the Greek language and it means the "end times," or the "doctrine of the last things." It connotes the part of systematic theology which deals with the final destiny both of the individual soul and of humankind.

Aramaic Idioms and Metaphors

One of the major challenges in understanding the 24th chapter of Matthew is that we have interpreted literally what were merely idiomatic and figurative sayings. By knowing Aramaic idioms and metaphors, we can unlock many phrases that Jesus used when he spoke of this great impending event.

Always with us

It is important to realize that the Bible does not speak of "two" comings, for the proper biblical term is "the coming of Christ." Interestingly, Matthew reports that Christ never left this world: "And behold I am with all of you always (all the days) even until the end of the world."[2] The powerful, transforming presence and consciousness of the living Christ is always with those who love truth and who practice the simple teachings of love and justice. These teachings are practical, universal principles applicable to everyone.

Matthew also reports to us in the gospel: "And when Jesus sat down on the Mount of Olives, his disciples drew near talking among themselves and they asked him: Tell us when will these things happen and what is the sign of your coming and of the end of the age?"[3] Jesus then described to his apostles three great happenings: (1) The fall and destruction of the holy city and temple under the Roman Prince Titus; (2) The success and triumph of his kingdom gospel—that is, the reigning presence of the Christ; (3) The end of the age (world). Jesus had answered

---

[2]Mt. 28:20, Aramaic Peshitta text.

[3]Mt. 24:3, Aramaic Peshitta text.

123

his disciples in very graphic language and told them of the events that would precede his coming.

The Coming

"Coming" in this passage implies in English "to come into your own." His disciples wondered when Jesus would bring his rule over the kingdoms of this world. At that time his disciples did not see or comprehend the spiritual mission of their lord. They reasoned in literal and political terms and understood everything materially, not spiritually. The apostles envisioned themselves reigning in the messianic, political kingdom with their master as king and themselves as twelve typical Eastern princes with large harems. Because they were very zealous to see King Herod dethroned, Rome defeated, and the messianic kingdom established, they asked Jesus for the sign of his success (coming).

The Warning

Jesus told them the following signs using Aramaic metaphors and idioms that are peculiar to the Near Eastern style of speaking and writing. According to Matthew, Jesus instructed them saying: "Immediately after the suffering of those days [the destruction of the temple, the fall of Jerusalem and the great suffering that the inhabitants would endure], the sun will become dark and the moon will not give its light and the stars will fall from the sky and the powers of the universe will be shaken."[4]

"The sun will be darkened and the moon will not give its light" is a Semitic poetic way of saying that the universe is to mourn over the tragic events that will take place on the earth. "Stars" symbolize political and religious leadership. Thus, when Jesus said that the stars would fall from the sky, he indicated that there would be changes in the government, political forces would be shaken, a complete change in ruling powers. Jesus also told his disciples: "Then the sign of this Human Being will be seen in the sky and all the generations of the earth will mourn and they will see this Human Being on the clouds of the sky."[5]

The above is typical Semitic, apocalyptic poetry that describes his "coming." "The sign of this Human Being will be seen in the sky" means that the followers of Christ will know of his coming through a revelation. The term "sky" refers to a high spiritual consciousness—that is, a consciousness which is alert to the sudden change that is about to take place.

His apocalyptic disclosure continues: "And all the generations of the earth will mourn, and they will see this Human Being coming on the clouds of the sky with power and great glory." "Coming on the clouds of the sky" means "to succeed in a mission" or "to be highly acclaimed and successful." In those days, the writers used the "clouds" as a figure of speech to suggest one had achieved the greatest heights ever. It was also believed that God rode the clouds as one would ride a chariot. Jesus, therefore, would eventually triumph all over the world. His power and presence, which is really the power and presence of God, would be realized and recognized among all nations.

---

[4]Mt. 24:29, Aramaic Peshitta text.

[5]Mt. 24:30, Aramaic Peshitta text.

The Announcement

"And he will send his angels with a large trumpet, and they will gather his chosen ones from the four winds, from one end of heaven to the other." "Large trumpet" signifies "an urgent and important announcement." The term "angels" refers to God's message (thoughts), God's counsel, intuitive guidance. "Four winds" denotes the four corners of the earth, and the phrase "from one end of the heaven to the other" means "from everywhere." The chosen will come from everywhere, from all over the earth.

Only One Coming

We have learned that the term "second coming" is not a biblical term. There is, and always has been, only one coming of the Christ referred to in Scripture. The man Jesus revealed the Christ in himself for all humanity, and what was once a mystery, hidden from the eyes of humankind, was then made known by his appearance. When Jesus spoke of his "coming," he used metaphorical and apocalyptic Near Eastern poetry to describe the universal conclusion of his gospel of the king-dom.[6] We also have learned the meanings of the idioms, symbols, and figurative Aramaic terms that appear in the 24th chapter of Matthew.

In the book of Acts, we find another passage that refers to his coming: "And they say to them, O Galilean men, Why are you here staring up at the sky? This very Jesus who has gone up from among you into heaven will come in the same way that you

---

[6]See Mk. 1:14-15.

have seen him and as he has ascended into heaven."[7] By the time this event occurred, the apostles had undergone a tremendous perceptual shift. A deep change had taken place within them. They had risen in consciousness. His disciples saw Jesus' ascension with transformed eyes. He arose in a spiritual body, free of space and time, although he had appeared to them in a way they formerly had known him.

The Final Appearance

Thus, the final coming of the Christ will be a spiritual manifestation free from all physical limitations. During this time, the consciousness of humanity will have been raised to a spiritual level so that every eye will see nothing but good. Humankind will realize its spiritual life and the entire world will recognize the Christ.

Revelation tells us that the kingdoms of this world are to become the kingdom of the Lord God and his Anointed (Christ). So, in the final stages of his coming, the glory and power of truth and justice will reign freely and joyously all over the earth. Love and nonviolence will have triumphed. Micah, the prophet, tells us: "And he will judge between many people, and rebuke strong nations afar off; and they will beat their swords into plowshares, and their spears into sickles; nation will not lift up sword against nation, neither will they learn war anymore. But they will sit every man under his vine and under his fig tree; and there will be none to harm them; for the mouth of the Lord of hosts has spoken it. For all people will walk everyone in the name of his god, and we will walk in the name of the Lord our

---

[7]Acts 1:11, Aramaic Peshitta text.

God forever and ever."[8]

A final note: There are numerous passages of Scripture throughout the entire New Testament that treat the theme of the so-called "Second Coming" of the Christ. Keep in mind that this chapter is not an exhaustive or comprehensive study of the Coming of the Christ. I merely present some ideas for consideration from the Aramaic language.

---

[8]Mic. 4:3-5, Aramaic Peshitta text.

19

Behold the King of the Universe

The seer Zechariah, through a prophetic vision, saw the coming of the Messiah. He uttered his prediction about the Messiah hundreds of years before the birth of Jesus. He saw that a meek spiritual leader would rule in God's kingdom. This Hebrew prophet declared his message boldly and openly when he said: "Rejoice exceedingly, O daughter of Zion! O daughter of Jerusalem! Look here, your King comes to you; he is just and a savior, meek and riding upon an ass, upon a colt the foal of an ass."[1]

Fulfillment

Approximately five hundred years later, Jesus of Nazareth instructed two of his disciples to go to Bethphage where they would find a donkey that was tied to a post and a colt with her. They were to bring the animals to him. "And they brought the donkey and the colt, and they put their garments on the colt, and Jesus rode upon it. And a very large crowd spread its garments on the road. Others cut down branches from the trees and spread them on the road. And the crowds that were going before him, and behind him, were shouting and saying: Victory to the son of David! Blessed is he who comes in the name of the Lord!

---

[1]Zech. 9:9, Aramaic Peshitta text.

Victory in the Highest!"[2]

Near Eastern Custom

In the Near East only the very poor would ride on a donkey—never princes and noblemen—because the ass usually signified disgrace, rejection, and humiliation. In many towns in the Near East today where old traditions prevail, the ancient custom of parading a disgraced person on an ass is still practiced. Any individual whose teaching was heretical, or who might have been immoral in character, was punished and abased in this manner.

The Objective of Jesus

Jesus chose the colt to ride into Jerusalem for a specific reason. He did not want to be received as an earthly, political leader or king. He represented the old ideas of ancient rulers of Israel who had lived among the people in meekness and humility and not as overlords. Jesus also knew that the priestly authorities would disgrace him and that his death was near. These priests would accuse him of blasphemy and so he would die the death of a common criminal on the cross. His destiny as a ruler of the world was not along political lines—his destiny lay in another direction.

Jesus' entry into Jerusalem was a political failure but, on the other hand, it was a moral and spiritual victory. The poor, the peasants, and the children welcomed him, but the high officials

---

[2]Mt. 21:7-9, Aramaic Peshitta text.

rejected him. In spite of this rejection, Jesus succeeded in demonstrating the nonpolitical, nonmaterial, and nonpartisan kingdom in his actions and in his teachings. His entry into the holy city struck a devastating blow to any political aspirations of his disciples. It collapsed the dreams and hopes for a militant leader to solve the problems of Israel, or the world. The picture that Jesus represented and demonstrated had nothing to do with political influence or military might. Behold, the king of the universe rides *triumphantly* upon a colt, a foal of an ass!

Its Meaning for Today

Spiritual values and attributes constitute a healthy, whole-some, balanced life. No kingdom or nation can survive or know the ultimate in peace and joy until spiritual values are estab-lished in that nation or kingdom. Genuine prosperity comes from the being of an individual. Material things come and go and are abundant one day and short the next. But the eternal values of the human spirit are from everlasting to everlasting. God's kingdom has no political ties with any particular nation or people. It belongs to the people of all nations. Wisdom and peace reign freely in God's kingdom. When heavenly wisdom and power dominate the leadership of this world, then and only then will everlasting peace and prosperity manifest all over the world.

20

The Power and Triumph of the Cross

I wrote this chapter as a dramatization. The intent is to bring the reader to the final scene of the crucifixion. However, this dramatization not only contains a description of the final events of the crucifixion and the emotional response of Jesus' apostles and disciples; it also teaches the meaning of the cross and the resurrection for us today.

The Drama

It was late afternoon and a strange, unnatural darkness had begun to blanket the little hill of Golgotha and all of Southern Palestine. The only lights one could see were the flickering lamps from the great holy city of Jerusalem, the shepherds' fires in the countryside, and the far off fires on the other side of the Jordan valley. There was a feeling of gloom everywhere.

Most of the people had already left the tragic scene of the crucifixion and the rest were beginning to take their leave. There were only a few newcomers remaining, mostly shepherds and farmers who had been unable to come earlier. Some of the priests and scribes still remained near the cross. A few Galileans were waiting to bury their beloved leader and teacher.

The victims on the cross were expected to die at any moment, but life seemed to linger for these three unfortunate ones. Sabbath was approaching and burial must be completed before sundown in accordance with religious law. The priests and elders were worried that the men would not die before the

Sabbath. They were very anxious for death to do its work.

Jesus' wounds were covered with flies and other insects. His body was weakening rapidly. At times he appeared as though he were already dead, but then he would move his head and look at the diminishing crowd. The pain of the crucifixion itself seemed to lessen as death slowly spread over his physical form.

Jesus once more became the target of insults. Some of the taunters shouted: "Your blood be upon your own head! You have trusted in God, let him deliver you!" His revilers were not content to see him dying this horrible death. They wanted to inflict new wounds upon him, wounds that neither sword, spear, nor arrow could inflict—wounds of scorn, bitterness, and blasphemy. These painful verbal arrows pierced his soul.

In that dark hour Jesus had no comforters. No one dared to speak a good word about him. His own disciples and followers were bewildered, not knowing what to make of this sudden turn of events. They had been hoping for a triumphant leader. They had hoped that the kingdom would be restored to Israel and their Master-Teacher crowned lord of lords and king of kings. Everything now looked hopeless and discouraging.

The life in their loving teacher was ebbing, and the expectation of a miracle was disappearing. Doubt was increasing in their hearts and minds. Jesus perceived that some of his followers shared in the doubts of his enemies, and he cried in a loud voice: *'el, 'el, l'mana shawakthani*! "O God, O God, to what a purpose you have kept me!" Or, according to the Lamsa translation of the Aramaic text: "My God, my God, for this was my destiny!"[1]

The remaining spectators rushed toward the cross. A

---

[1]See Rocco A. Errico, *Let There Be Light: The Seven Keys*, "Was Jesus Forsaken?" pp. 12-17.

puzzled look appeared on the faces of the scribes and priests wondering what that strange utterance could mean? Some said he had called on Elijah for help. Others became tense, as though expecting Elijah to appear and perform a miracle. But the Galileans who were standing near the cross knew Jesus did not cry for Elijah to save him. They understood his words that were uttered in the Galilean dialect of Aramaic. It was a cry of victory and not of despair or desperation.

Now as the disciples were watching this scene and heard those words of triumph, they began to recall all that their lord had told them about his suffering and death. They understood that his cry was uttered as a consolation for them. It was a cry of affirmation of his mission. A mission that revealed meekness and love. It unmasked the face of death and unveiled the mysteries of life that would liberate men, women, and children throughout the entire world.

The end was nearing and suddenly Jesus cried out: "It is fulfilled." All the prediction concerning the Messiah had come to fulfillment. Its final chapter was written on the hill of Golgotha. Jesus completed his work and finished the prophecies. He had revealed God as a loving and forgiving parent. He had proved his teachings, not with mere words of logic and philosophy, but by living and demonstrating his truth. His earthly ministry of preaching was vividly and dramatically summarized in a few hours on the cross. This was the end of Jesus' suffering but not the end of his life. He was soon to manifest God's power through his death and bring life and immortality to light.

The two criminals who had been crucified with Jesus occasionally uttered some confused remarks, calling on their relatives for water, or complaining of their wounds and the bitter end that they had met.

Jesus had been silent now for quite some time. His eyes

were closed and his body was motionless. Some were saying that he was dead. Others were saying that he was dying, still others expected another cry before his end would come. The body of Jesus moved once again. His face was completely colorless. He slowly opened his eyes and spoke, but this time his voice could scarcely be heard. "Father, into your hands I surrender my spirit." Throughout all of his suffering he had not said a word of disappointment, nor even expressed a word of doubt. Death finally removed Jesus from his agony on the cross.

It was late Friday evening. The soldiers were drawing near the crosses, one of them with a hammer in his hand. A few people gathered near the dead men. One of the soldiers began breaking the legs of the criminals to be sure they were dead. When that soldier came to Jesus, he could see that he was already dead. But he took his spear and pierced Jesus' side and gazed at the face of the victim to see if there were any signs of life. Jesus never felt the spear. His spirit was totally in the hands of his Father. Some water and blood flowed from his pierced side.

Jesus' body was hastily removed from the cross and was wrapped with a white linen cloth that one of his followers had provided. But the complete burial would have to wait until the Sabbath was over. The body was to be anointed with spices and given a permanent resting place. None of the disciples dreamed that the tomb would be found empty when they returned to complete his burial on the first day of the week.

Soon, these disciples were to awaken to a revelation of life that would forever transform them. They were soon to know the power and victory of the cross. They were to learn that no grave could hold the living Christ. His body was to be the first fruit of the resurrection that would awaken humankind to the realization of life eternal. The consciousness of humanity would now transcend its earthly boundaries and encompass a complete and limitless heavenly order of life.

The symbol of the cross that had always been the symbol of finality and total annihilation was to become the symbol of life and glory. This cross was to be known as the way of enlightenment and nonviolent way of life. Jesus' teaching brought him to the cross. He had impressed on the minds of his disciples the fact that death would not be the end of his mission but the beginning of a new spiritual era, the inauguration of a heavenly order. It is no wonder the apostle Paul so clearly exclaimed in his letter to the Corinthians: "O death, where is your sting? O grave, where is your victory? But thanks be to God who gives us the victory through our Lord Jesus the Messiah!"

21

New Tongues

"And he [Jesus] said to them: Go into all the world and proclaim my joyful message [gospel] to the whole creation. . . Then these signs will follow those who believe these things. In my name they will heal the insane; and they will speak with new tongues. . . "[1]

Northern Aramaic

Jesus taught and preached in his own native language of Aramaic. His particular dialect was the Northern, Near Eastern, Galilean form of Aramaic. (Today biblical scholars call this language East Syriac. However, the term "Syriac" is a misnomer. Since Jesus spoke in Galilean Aramaic, he used many Northern idioms to express his ideas.)

In the above scriptural quotation Jesus expressed several idioms: "in my name," which means "according to my way or method"; "to cast out devils," which denotes healing the mentally ill." "They will speak with new tongues" suggests two ideas. The first idea is that Jesus' disciples were soon to speak the languages of other races and peoples. God's spirit would help them learn and speak the new tongues that were unknown and strange to them. The second idea is that in the Near East when news of peace or a joyful and wonderful declaration is proclaimed, it is often called "a new tongue." "To speak in new

---

[1]Mk. 16:15-17, Aramaic Peshitta text.

tongues" is to declare a loving, peaceful, and joyful message full of hope. An opposite notion is true when the people use the idiom "to speak in a strange tongue." When a Semitic ruler admonishes his subjects, the people often say: "He speaks in a strange tongue."

The Apostle Paul

Paul also made use of this idiom when he wrote: "Though I speak with the tongues of men and angels and have not love in my heart, I am become as sounding brass, or a tinkling cymbal."[2] "Tongues of men" simply means "common, ordinary speech." "Tongues of angels" refers to "a truthful, sincere language" or "speech without deceit or deception." Thus, Paul tells us that love is what gives a genuine quality to our words and deeds.

---

[2] 1 Cor. 13:1, Aramaic Peshitta text.

PART TWO

Commentaries
Here and There in Scripture

22

The Meaning of Religion

Our English word *religion* comes directly from the Latin language. Its Latin root is *religare* (*re*, "re," and *ligare*, "to tie" or "to bind;" thus it means "to retie or rebind"). Biblical writers often use the term "way" or "the way of God" to indicate *religion*. A common expression one often finds in the Hebrew Bible is "walk ye in the way of the Lord." This phrase means "obey the laws of God" or "walk in the ways of God." The Aramaic word for "way" is *urha*.

According to the gospel of John, Jesus used this term *urha* ("way," "path," or "road") when he said "I am the *way*, the truth and the life."[1] What John emphasizes is that Jesus' teaching is the way to know God as the Father of all humanity. His Galilean Master-Teacher opened the way for everyone.

Deyna in Aramaic is another term for "religion." This same Aramaic word means "balance," "judgment," "equity," and "order." Religion, then, is a *way* of life that brings order, balance, peace, and harmony into our lives. Religion leads us to our essential and genuine selves. Through religion we come to know the abiding, living presence we call God. For God indwells our hearts and minds. It is one thing to know about the God of holy Scripture, but it is another matter to discern the God of our souls.

A practical religion works with metaphysical ideas of God, the universe, and nature. The intellect alone cannot fully comprehend metaphysical laws that govern the uni-verse. We

---

[1]Jn. 14:6.

141

also need our intuition and imagination to explore the spiritual laws that regulate our world and that direct our hearts and minds.

The human faculties of intuition and imagination are the channels through which all great religions have come to us. We refer to this particular phenomenon as mysticism. But we typically think of mysticism as something strange and impractical.

Nonetheless, mysticism is a spiritual practice whereby we may gain understanding through subjective, intuitive experience. It is a *knowing* that goes beyond any ordinary perception of life and becomes a transcendental realization. It is through this particular heightened awareness that we can sense the ordinary world from a more sensitive position and perspective. The rational mind alone cannot perceive the invisible patterns and hidden order of the universe. It takes the nonrational area of mind to reveal what is hidden.

Religion as Balance

When we bring ourselves into harmony and balance with the universe and its spiritual principles, we then can live in the true joy of genuine religion. This kind of religion is never the subject of controversy, because it is not doctrinal or creedal. What brings us into balance is the realization that true religion is based on the principles of life, love, peace, justice, and an all-inclusiveness. It does not create a "special few" or insiders and outsiders. This form of religion is pure and needs no temples, shrines, or special priesthood to administer it.

Most of the discord and strife usually blamed on religion comes from man-made doctrines and dogmas. Customs and religious ordinances are simply empty gestures. These things are like wells without water and clouds that appear full of rain but which never water the dry earth. A spiritual religion, however, creates great joy, abundant peace, and a healthy, harmonious style of living. It frees us from a judgmental attitude of others.

Religion of the Heart

A heartfelt religion is a function of life and is just as important and essential to the soul as water, air, and sun are to the physical body. All races have some form of religious order. Even the most primitive tribal people feel the emanation of an omnipresence, a mysterious power in the universe from which they seek guidance and protection. No race is ever left without some heavenly revelation and guidance. This is because a human being is akin to God. "And God said let us make man in our image, after our likeness. . ."[2] Humanity, according to the Hebrew Bible, is the image and expression of its Creator. Therefore, humanity's essence is eternal, universal, and cannot be separated from God. However, we may, through erroneous thinking, separate ourselves from God. Nevertheless, the soul always seeks to know its source.

From time immemorial, the human family has felt the power of nature's hidden forces within and without. Humanity craves a world free of war, famine, conflict, and violence. If such a world order were not possible, I believe, we human beings would never aspire to know such an existence.

People, in attempting to meet everyday challenges, have tried every conceivable form of worship from crude primitive

---

[2]Gen. 1:26, KJV.

143

ceremonies to the pomp and grandeur of rituals and temples. At times fears, debts, calamities, sickness, and death have compelled people to turn to spiritual forces and to seek understanding from a much larger reality than just the things that normal reasoning can grasp. Challenges will always be with us, but we do not have to solve them with violence. Revealed religion aids us in our quest for peace and harmony.

It appears to be humankind's nature to worship something. If one does not care to worship God, then one will worship something else. We might worship money, country, race, a marital partner, or even ourselves. It is true that men and women, because of their divine origin, have a capacity for deep devotion and high aspiration. However, at times this devotion is misused and results in the creation of many mistaken religious notions.

Two Types of Religion

We can divide religion into two categories: (1) A revealed religion that is intrinsic, coming from the soul of humanity; (2) A formal religion that is man-made. The first is real, eternal, unchangeable, and transcends all material forms of worship. The second is temporal, changeable, and bound by cultural customs and human tradition.

Every child born into this world is endowed with spiritual energies that develop as he or she grows. Even in childhood the religion of the soul is inherent because the soul is neither young nor old. Jesus said: "Allow the little children to come to me and do not hold them back; because the sovereign counsel of heaven is *for such as these.*"[3]

Most of what we call religion today is obtained through adoption and is born out of the clash of cultures and ideas. Since religion is a reality, it is natural for the human family to be born religious and unnatural to adopt a formal religion which is contrary to its intuition and inner understanding. Sometimes choices of different formal religions are made out of certain conveniences rather than from a deep inner conviction. For example, one may choose a formal religion for a better social status in the community. Then, again, we must realize that birth and environment have a great deal to do with shaping one's formal religion.

When children are born, they are free from all man-made laws, ordinances, and doctrines. Children know nothing about the religion of their parents. Boys and girls essentially see no difference between themselves and other children with whom they may play. However, once children learn the man-made rules and regulations from their parents whom they love and trust, then they may maintain a mistaken attitude toward the creeds and beliefs of others whom they do not know or trust.

It is impossible for us to create an ideology and a system of worship and then genetically transmit them to our children. Every generation comes into this world free of fear, falsehood, and superstition. A simple, revealed religion is all-inclusive and infinite, but a man-made religion is exclusive and finite.

Religion is not to please or appease a deity, as some believe. It is for the benefit of the entire human family. When we practice justice, love of neighbors, and forgiveness of ourselves and others, the world then becomes a peaceful place in which to live.

---

[3]Mt. 19:14, Aramaic Peshitta text.

145

God needs no worshipers. Neither has God ever been in need of sacrifices, offerings, or ceremonies. The slaying of animals or human beings for worship and forgiveness of sins was never God's idea. Violence is not the way of God to cure human ills. The Hebrew prophets made this very clear. (See for example Jeremiah 7:21-23, Isaiah 1:11-20; 66:1-3, Hosea 6:6; 8:13, Amos 5:25 and Ezekiel 33:7-11.) God is in need of nothing. We are the ones who are in need. The entire earth—all nature—gives glory to God, and when we give glory and honor to God, we transcend a personal sense of self.

Truth—Another Name for God

Truth is another name for God. Truth is inherent, intrinsic, and natural to all of us. But we must learn to discern truth on a daily basis—that is, from moment to moment so that we may apply it to our lives. The phenomenon of a church is better understood when we realize that it is a place to celebrate the truth of life.

Interestingly, the word for church in Aramaic not only means "a gathering place" but also means "to throw a party." It is not just a place to learn but also a place to practice and demonstrate a better order of life. A church becomes a spiritually disciplined society that celebrates living. The objective of a true religion is to give humanity a just and workable social order. Religion is to serve us and not we religion.

23

The Human-Divine Paradigm

I have often been asked: "Where would one begin in the study of Scripture, especially if one's approach was not just a Biblical historical search? And, where would one begin if the goal was about the context of being or existence? My usual reply is that one must begin with an understanding of God and not just with the Bible.

We can only initiate an understanding of life, being, and existence when we learn what is the context of our existence. There are four existential questions we need to address. Who are we? What are we? Where are we? What is our purpose? People who are searching for understanding and enlightenment usually ask these four common existential questions. To answer them we start with the idea of *knowing* God. But, then, we may ask: Is God knowable? And, what do we mean when we use the word "know?"

Knowing God

To know God means more than just an intellectual definition that satisfies a curious mind. *Knowing* God is more than a conceptual idea about God. God is not an idea. Ideas, definitions and concepts are helpful but are not ends in themselves. They point to truth. We need ideas and definitions to help us communicate, but the real meaning of *knowing* is beyond words and symbols. It takes a genuine, living realization of God in our hearts, minds, and bodies to know God. (For a detailed understanding of the Aramaic and Hebrew verb "to know," see Part Two, chapter 27, "The Power of Knowing.")

A Prayer for Knowing God

In the 17th chapter of John's gospel, we find a farewell prayer attributed to Jesus.[1] The gospel writer has Jesus praying: "And this is life forever: that they might know that you are the one true God, the one who sent Jesus the Messiah."[2] Jesus' disciples had to come to a living realization of knowing God for themselves and we also must come to the same realization. He continues in the prayer "I am not making this request for these alone, but also for the sake of those who believe in me through their word."[3] Again, John has Jesus praying for future adherents to his teaching.

Knowing God is truly "life forever." The mystery of life and its subtle forces are revealed to us when we realize that God is our very life center and energy. Jesus revealed the truth that God is knowable. At another time, Jesus said: "Delighted are

---

[1] According to most NT scholars, a redactor (editor) of John's gospel added this prayer from an independent composition when he also added chapters 15 and 16. Raymond E. Brown suggests that "Perhaps the prayer came from the same circle within the Johannine church that produced the Prologue, for the two works have interesting similarities in their poetic quality, careful structure, and theme." Be that as it may, the editor drew on synoptic gospel parallels. He also expanded upon traditional sayings of Jesus. See Raymond E. Brown, THE GOSPEL OF JOHN, XII — XXI, vol. 2, pp. 744 - 748.

[2] Jn 17:3, Aramaic Peshitta text.

[3] Jn. 17:20, Aramaic Peshitta text.

those who are pure in their hearts [sincere—those who have a clear mind] for they will see [perceive] God."[4]

What Is God?

But, we may ask, what is God? The Aramaic word for God is *Alaha* and it comes from the Semitic root *el*. It describes *something* or a *presence* that *sustains* and *supports*. Remember, we cannot fully define God, but we can know God. God is beyond functional thought but not out of the reach of human consciousness or the sensitivity of our hearts and souls.

Many deep experiences in life are extremely difficult to define or capture with words alone. For instance, how can we explain with mere words the depth of love and care a mother and father have for their children? Or how can we account for the mysterious bond of love? Love defies definition. In reality, almost anything of a profoundly deep nature challenges definition. There exist certain realizations which occur in human consciousness that we cannot fully comprehend, but we can apprehend them. This applies to knowing God.[5] Again in John's gospel, we read about an episode between Jesus and a Samaritan woman.

God Is Spirit

Jesus says to the woman: "For God is spirit; and those who

---

[4]Mt. 5:8, Aramaic Peshitta text.

[5]For further information on the meaning of God, see Rocco A. Errico, *The Mysteries of Creation: The Genesis Story*, pp. 46-60.

worship him must worship him in spirit and in truth."[6] Rooha, "spirit," has many meanings in Aramaic.[7] In this particular scriptural passage it means "Intelligence." (Thus God is Intelligence—the life force that is everywhere and in everything. It is an Intelligent Power that cannot be confined anywhere.)

John, in his first epistle, tells us more about what God is in essence and what it means to know God. "My beloved, let us love one another; for love is from God; and everyone who loves is born of God and *knows God*. He who does not love *does not know God*: For God is love."[8] Through both of these scriptures, one from John's gospel and the other from John's epistle, we can see that God is Intelligence (Spirit) and Love, hence Love-Intelligence.

Anyone who is loving knows God. Love is more than an emotion. Love is God in motion. God is love and love is God. "See how abundant the love of the Father is toward us, for he has called us children and made us: therefore the world does not know us because it did not know him. My beloved, now we are the children of God [love]."[9]

Who and What Are We?

Children of God (Love-Intelligence) is who we are. Love-Intelligence is what constitutes our beings. When we begin with God we begin with the one and only true and genuine image of

---

[6]Jn. 4:24, Aramaic Peshitta text.

[7]See Part 2, Chapter 10, "Rooha—Spirit."

[8]1 Jn. 4:7-8, Aramaic Peshitta text.

[9]1 Jn. 3:1-2, Aramaic Peshitta text.

ourselves—Love-Intelligence. The Torah explicitly expresses this idea and answers the question of who and what we are. The creation story author gives us a spiritual picture and the authentic context of our beings:

"Then God said: Let us make humankind in our image, as our resemblance. Let them have dominion over the fish of the sea, and over the winged creatures of the sky, over the animals, over all the wild land beasts, and over all the reptiles that creep on the earth. So God created humankind in his image, in the image of God, he created them, male and female, he created them."[10] This is the human-divine paradigm. It is the pattern of humankind, humanity created in the divine image. This image appears to be latent in most of humanity and not active. Jesus of Nazareth came to restore this image and to refresh our memories of who we are. In John's gospel we read the following: "But to those who accept him [his teaching] to them he gave the right [authority, power] to become children of God, especially those who believe in his name [his authority and teaching]."[11]

Male and Female

The inspired writer of the creation epic also tells us that both male and female are the image of God. According to the text, one is not superior and the other inferior. After all, how can one aspect of God's image be inferior to another? Metaphysically, male and female are spiritual qualities in both men and women. Every individual is complete in herself or himself. God's image is complete and fulfilled, perfect and harmonious

---

[10]Gen.. 1:26-27, Aramaic Peshitta text.

[11]Jn. 1:12, Aramaic Peshitta text.

in everyone. The only difference is that some have realized this truth in their lives and others have not yet awakened to this powerful unfoldment and realization of themselves.

We are God's children. No one individual can be totally equal with God in quantity—all powerful and everywhere. We are equal in quality—that is, of the same essence. So many religious leaders believe that God is too holy for sinful and unclean human beings to even approach this Deity, let alone that we are his children. Nonetheless, our true identity is God's image.

I use the expression "true identity" not in opposition to a "false identity" but from the Latin meaning of this word "true." In Latin the word is *Verus* and it means "that which is." The real identity crisis most of us experience today is not one of a particular role in life but it is an existential one — a spiritual crisis. We suffer from metaphysical anxiety because we fail to realize our fundamental oneness with life, i.e., God. Our suffering over identity persists until we awaken to the essential order of who and what we are in essence. It is realization alone, on an acute inner level of awareness, and not just an intellectual belief or exercise that will heal us.

Identification

We may also understand the answer to the questions of who and what we are by knowing who we are not. We identify so strongly with our cherished and projected "images" of ourselves that it becomes increasingly challenging for us to recognize who we really are. For example our names may be "Mary," "Elaine," "Robert," "David," and so forth, but these "identification tags" are only handy labels of classification and are not the true essence of our beings. Our so-called "ethnic origins" also set up barriers that obstruct us from seeing who we really are.

I have not even mentioned our ingrained and entrenched identification with our revered "religious beliefs" and centuries of cultural "traditions." In themselves there is nothing "wrong" with these identifications except that we must begin to see through them. I only refer to them as hindrances that block us from totally perceiving what really is. Once we recognize that we are none of these "identifications" then the energy and truth of who and what we are clearly emerge from within us.

Divine Consciousness

As human beings we are manifestations of divine con-sciousness. We are humanly divine and divinely human! We are spirit in bodily form. We are what Jesus once declared to the listeners of his day—children of the most High. He had just told the people that he and his Father were of one accord. "I and my Father are one." Some of the people in his audience did not like what he said. So they began to pick up stones for they were wanting to stone him.

Jesus' response to their reactions was as follows: "I have shown you many good works from my Father; for which one of them do you stone me?" Their conduct was not because of his good works but because he blasphemed. They said: "For while you are only a man, you make yourself God." But Jesus answered them saying: "Is it not so written in your Torah — I said, You are gods?" John has Jesus quoting Psalm 82:6 that says: "I have said, You are gods; all of you are children of the most High."

Regardless of whether Jesus actually said these words or

not, they probably do go back to Jesus' understanding and divine awareness about humanity. He also knew that humankind had unwittingly suppressed its divine image and likeness.

In Philippians 2:5-6, Paul says: "Reason this within you which Jesus the Messiah also reasoned, who, being in the form of God, did not consider it robbery to be equal with God." Jesus understood his relationship with God. He based his action upon his awareness of his Father, therefore, he knew who and what he was. He also knew that humanity would have to come to this awareness for there to be universal peace and harmony.

We may constantly reason that we are *just* men and women. Usually calculative thinking rationalizes us out of recognizing our right to our relationship with God as children of the divine. When we judge strictly by appearances and experiences, we generally blind ourselves to what really is. Jesus' critics were a perfect example of the "religious" rational mind of the time.

But, we may ask, since we are a manifestation of divine consciousness, then what is divine consciousness? Let us consider what divine consciousness is not. It is not just physical awareness—conscious only of pleasure and pain or states of sensation. It is not just personal self-awareness—awareness of personal mind and life with its so-called racial or ethnic "roots." It is not just interpersonal consciousness—awareness of interaction with others, interpersonal relationships. It is not time consciousness—awareness of past, present, or future. It is not just intellectual consciousness—awareness of knowledge composed of opinions and theories.

Divine consciousness is a spiritual awareness that observes the entire spectrum of the phenomenal world, that is, the world of appearances. This world of appearances cannot deceive the spiritual mind. Divine awareness sees through the facade of the world. It does not focus or lock on the physical, personal, interpersonal, time or intellectual projections of the mind. These varied levels of mind cannot fascinate or captivate divine consciousness. It understands and perceives them for what they are. They are only appearances and experiences. It knows them to be ephemeral and not what truly *is*.

Divine consciousness is a loving consciousness that does not create guilt or blame. It is open and receptive. It always responds to life and it is exactly what God is. This spiritual awareness realizes love, peace, joy, and goodness.

Our socio-cultural thinking conditions most of us but when we begin to know our true identity and origin, we free ourselves from that conditioning. As we identify with life and existence from their true source, then we spontaneously manifest their nature and reality. Truth always is and, therefore, validates itself. Truth needs no defense. It is the only reality that is. Truth is not a doctrine. It is life itself and it is beyond all forms of classification and appearances.

Where Are We?

Most of us know where we are situated on this planet we call earth. But we really don't know exactly where the earth is located. Actually, there isn't a scientist anywhere that can honestly tell us where we are. The earth, being somewhere in a tremendous universe of galaxies, has no starting point from which to measure. At least, we can't seem to find any definitive starting point.

All that we are certain about is the fact that we are on this planet we have named "earth." We also know that earth is somewhere in a vast, expanding universe. Knowing where we are geographically is not the answer to our question, where are we? The following is from my book on the Genesis Story:

Psychologically we feel we know where we are because we have named the area, or the place, in which we reside. We also feel comfortable by setting parameters. However, naming a place and setting boundaries does not really tell us where we are. For instance, when one crosses the border from Arizona to California, the land does not know it has been divided and its name changed. Naming places and things is a convenience we have invented out of necessity to simplify communication and to locate things and ourselves. The reality is this: places and things are nameless. To quote Max Muller, philosopher, "things are thinks."

There are those, of course, who attempt to answer philosophically and religiously the question, "Where are we?" Often, when I lecture on the subject of creation, I ask my listeners to answer this question for me. The audience is generally quick to reply with learned, metaphysical, or philosophical conditioned responses such as: "We are here," "We are in God," "We are in the now, the present moment."

These responses usually engender more probing questions: "Where is here?" "Where in God?" "Where and what is the now?" All answers, no matter how plausible they may be to the rational mind, tend to dissipate as mere diversions when examined closely. They do not provide us with deeply satisfying solutions because this type of inquiry demands our entire being to participate in its resolve.

We cannot honestly and truly give an answer to "Where are we?" As unbelievable as this is going to seem to us, we have to face the inevitable fact that we are lost! It is, no doubt, utterly humbling for us to realize that we don't know where we are. Not only is this incredible to ponder, but it is just as staggering to imagine how our being is possible at all! In other words, our human presence is an enigma also!

156

If we deeply perceive this realization, it becomes the beginning of wisdom and the ending of arrogance. We are restored to a childlike state of wonder, inquisitiveness, sensitivity, and responsiveness to ourselves and everything around us.

We truly exist in a vast, expansive, mysterious universe of which we know so little in spite of our ever increasing knowledge in the fields of science, metaphysics, theology, archeology, and anthropology. Our state of being is a great mystery. Even our so-called "physical" forms are a great wonder and mystery to us. And what is so astounding is that our lives are also a mystery![12]

The Metaphysical Context

Having established the fact that literally we do not know where we are, at least we can partially understand our context from a metaphysical perspective. When the apostle Paul was at Athens debating in the market places with Greek philosophers who were of the teaching of Epicurus and others called Stoics, he made an amazing deduction. While present in the court at Areopagus, he addressed the men of Athens with the following:

I see that above all things you are extravagant in the worship of idols. For as I walked about, and viewed the house of your idols, I found an altar with this inscription: This is the altar of the unknown god. He therefore, while you know him not but yet worship him, is the very one I am preaching to you. . . . *FOR IN HIM WE LIVE AND MOVE*

---

[12]Rocco A. Errico, *The Mysteries of Creation: The Genesis Story,* "Where are we?", pp. 42-44. See also "Matter and Substance," pp. 44-45.

AND HAVE OUR BEING, as some of your own wise men have said, For we are his kindred.[13]

Thus on a transpersonal (spiritual) level, we understand ourselves to live in the context of God. In other words, we live, move and have our being in the omnipresent, Divine Love-Intelligence. When this realization dawns clearly in our minds and hearts then a new perception will take place. We will no longer "feel" bound to the earth or any particular location. When we realize that we live in God, our divine context, all limitation ceases. In the famous and often quoted Psalm, the writer tells what it means to live in a divine pattern:

> He who dwells in the protection of the Most High shall abide under the shadow of the Almighty. I will say of the LORD, he is my refuge and my fortress, my God. In him will I trust. Surely he shall deliver you from the snare of the fowler, and from vain gossip. He will cover you with his feathers, and under his wings you shall trust. His truth shall be your shield and buckler. You shall not be afraid for the terror by night nor for the arrow that flies by day, nor for the conspiracy that spreads in darkness, nor for the pestilence that wastes at noonday. Thousands shall fall at your side, and ten thousand at your right hand, but it shall not come near you. . . . For he shall give his angels charge over you to keep you in all your ways.[14]

An amplified rendering of verse one would read as follows: "He who rests in the secure, hidden place of the Most High will live under the protection of the Almighty." It is a secret place

---

[13]Acts 17:23-28, Aramaic Peshitta text, Lamsa translation.

[14]Ps. 91:1-7, 11, Aramaic Peshitta text, Lamsa translation.

because it is hidden from human eyes and understanding. It is not a geographical location but a state of consciousness. As we continue to make our home in God and realize we live in divine mind, we are protected wherever we are. This is the only secure place to live—in the consciousness of God's loving, nonviolent, healing presence!

What Is Our Purpose?

Let us look to the teaching of Jesus to see what he had to say about purpose in our lives. He taught his disciples saying:

> You have heard that it was said, Be friendly to your neighbor and hate your enemy. Yet I tell you: Love your enemies, bless anyone who curses you, do good to them who hate you, pray for those who oppress you and persecute you, So that you may be the children of your Father who is in heaven, he who lets his sun shine upon the good and upon the bad, and who lets his rain fall upon the just and the unjust. If, then you love only those who love you, what payment do you have? Look here, are not they, the tax collectors, also doing the same? And if you greet your brothers only, what more are you doing? Are not they, the tax collectors, also doing the same? Therefore, be all-inclusive even as your Father who is in heaven is all-inclusive.[15]

From Jesus' teaching we can readily see that our purpose in life is to be a nonviolent and loving presence. But, a loving presence does not make itself known out of sheer willfulness. A

---

[15]Mt. 5:43-48, Aramaic Peshitta text.

presence such as this manifests itself from a deep, inner spiritual realization of who, what, and where we are. This *knowing* comes from an intuitive, transcendental level of understanding. The intellectual mind is not the source of love, nor are the emotions the source of a loving presence.

In the King James Version of this verse of Jesus' teaching, the master says to his disciples: "Be perfect even as your Father in heaven is perfect." The Aramaic term *gmeera* means "perfect," "complete," "thorough," "finished," "mature," "full grown," and "all-inclusive." Thus, we may translate the words of Jesus to mean "all-inclusive."

A Loving Presence

This loving presence is all-inclusive. It recognizes no barriers, boundaries, race, color, or creed. God is good to all. Therefore, his "children" are also good to all. Children of God are sincere, wise, alert, gentle, and courageous. A loving presence is a mature presence. In his letter to the Corinthians, Paul aptly describes the essence of love.

> Love is patient and kind. Love does not envy. Love does not make a vain display of itself, and does not boast. Love does not behave itself unseemly, it seeks not its own, it is not easily provoked, and thinks no evil. Love rejoices not over iniquity, but rejoices in the truth. It bears all things, believes all things, hopes all things, endures all things. Love never comes to an end.[16]

A loving presence is a place where God is happening; that

---

[16]1 Cor. 13:4-8, Aramaic Peshitta text.

is, peace, joy, and harmony are manifesting. We cannot plan, calculate or personalize this kind of love. Love is transpersonal and it simply is! Calculative thinking cannot operate or function in the presence of love. God is Spirit. God is a living presence and not merely laws. Love, peace, joy, and harmony are the very essence and presence we call God. We are expressions and reflections of divine awareness that manifest this very presence. This is our metaphysical purpose in life.

We must not feel discouraged when we seem to manifest the opposite of truth. The manifestation of a "personal self" is only a mistaken idea in our thinking. The more we realize the only true Self, the more the loving presence manifests. We are becoming what we are in reality! Life is a divine revelation. The words of John encourage us to continue our growth as children of God and as revelators of the divine presence:

> See how abundant the love of the Father is toward us, for he has called us children and made us. My beloved, now we are the children of God and as yet it has not been revealed what we will be. But we know that when he will appear, we will be in his likeness. For we will see him as he is. Let everyone who has this hope in him purify himself, even as he is pure.[17]

---

[17] 1 Jn. 3:1-3, Aramaic Peshitta text.

161

24

Darkness

According to some writers of antiquity, the beginning of all things consisted of a dark mist, spiritual in nature, and of a turbid black chaos. Hebrew Scripture also presents this idea. "As for the earth it was chaos, and darkness was upon the deep (ocean). And the spirit of God hovered compassionately over the surface of the waters."[1]

Chapter one of Genesis depicts a scene of darkness and chaos. The author of this chapter sees the earth in a primitive state. All raw material and forces were present but unformed and latent; that is, it was not capable of supporting life eco-systems as we now know them. He describes a huge watery mass (ocean) enveloping a chaotic earth. Darkness was prevailing over everything, but at the same time some powerful life force was hovering over the surface of the waters.

The entire scene that the revelator describes vibrates with a compassionate, empathetic presence, an Intelligence. Then in the midst of the darkness, this loving Intelligence brought forth light. Darkness was suddenly energized from a hidden source. "Then God exclaimed: Let there be light! And there was light. Now God saw the light that it was beautiful. So God separated the light from the darkness. Then God named the light: Day. And he named the darkness: Night. . . ."[2] The appearance of

---

[1]Gen. 1:2, Aramaic Peshitta text.

[2]Gen. 1:4–5, Aramaic Peshitta text. Interestingly the sun, moon, and stars were not created until the fourth day. See Gen. 1:14–15.

light balanced the darkness which prevailed everywhere.

The Meaning of Black

Black, or the state of darkness, is not a curse, nor is it evil. There is nothing in this so-called material universe which is maleficent in and of itself. Metaphorically and metaphysically, we human beings have made the color *black* and *darkness* represent evil, disaster, sorrow, distress, ignorance, blindness, and superstition. This is strictly a relative point of view.

Blackness and darkness do represent something more than just the above-mentioned negative terms. Darkness holds many hidden wonders. In the blackness of the night, we are able to see the stars and study the heavens. In the darkness of the womb, human life is conceived and nurtured. In the darkness of the soil, seeds germinate. In the darkness of the mind, ideas are born. Darkness is nature's time of rest, formation, incubation, and secret rendezvous of invisible powers and unseen realities.

We usually teach that light and white are symbolic of God. But darkness and black symbolize God also. Darkness represents God as the Inscrutable Source, the Unknowable, and the Unmanifest. In Christian mysticism, the Supreme Reality first appears to the inner eye as darkness. This apparent darkness, however, is in itself light, dazzling and blinding in its splendor. It gradually becomes visible as such when spiritual vision becomes purged and purified.

Scripture tells us that light came into existence on the first day. But there is no word about the creation of darkness. This implies that darkness may have always existed. Thus, darkness also represents God as the Void. According to the ancient Egyptians, First Principle is characterized as darkness rather than light because it is beyond all human rationalization and calculation. Although we represent God as light, Genesis chapter one does not conceive of God as light. The author describes God as totally transcendental. God is above and beyond all concepts. This magnificent Power simply brings forth elements, deifying no heavenly or earthly element.

Darkness—God's Dwelling

Biblical authors at times refer to darkness in a higher, positive mode. They often depicted their Deity surrounded by darkness, clouds, and tempests. "And the Lord said to Moses, Lo, I am coming to you in a thick [dark, black] cloud. . . And it happened on the third day in the morning that there were thunders and lightning and a thick cloud. . ."[3]

Thunders represent power and truth; lightning denotes flashes of intuition and illumination. The psalmist says: "He [God] made darkness his secret shelter; his tent round about him was darkness of waters and thick clouds of the sky. "[4]

In the ancient days darkness was "the mystery of all mysteries." Therefore, sages and prophets describe God as dwelling in, and surrounded by, darkness. Life itself is also dark because its source is a mystery and inscrutable. Life is ever a mystery we cannot solve. But, it is a mystery we live and express continually.[5]

---

[3]Ex. 19:9, 16, Aramaic Peshitta text.

[4]Ps. 18:11, Aramaic Peshitta text.

[5]See Rocco A. Errico, *The Mysteries of Creation: The Genesis Story*, pp. 39–45 and pp. 86–91.

25

The Great Shepherd

In Hebrew Scripture there exists an incomparable beloved and celebrated psalm. It is one of the most quoted and highly cherished songs in the Bible. We call it the 23rd Psalm. This encouraging short psalm has dried many tears and has given troubled hearts a firm faith and tranquil trust.

Originally, the psalms were religious folk songs. They reflected the faith of the Hebrew people. As a nation, biblical Israel lived its life centered upon God. The 23rd psalm is a reassuring song that touches and comforts one's heart and soul. It very humanly portrays truth principles and metaphysical laws of joy, peace, and prosperity.

Before we contemplate this masterful poetic hymn, verse by verse, let us see how the psalm reads in the Aramaic Peshitta text. The following is my translation of the 23rd psalm from Aramaic:

The Lord[1] shepherds me and
I lack nothing at all!
And in pastures of strength
He makes me dwell.
He guides me by restful waters.

---

[1] The Hebrew text reads *YHWH — YAHWEH*. The Aramaic text reads *MARYAH* (LORD). Some scholars suggest that the Aramaic term *maryah* derives from two Aramaic words: *mar* ("lord") and the abbreviated form of the name of *yahweh* ("*yah.*") Thus, in Aramaic the term *maryah* may have originally meant "Lord Yah."

He has restored my life.
And upon pathways of justice
He leads me.
Because of your reputation,
even if I walk through the valleys
of the shadows of death,
I fear no danger
because you are with me.
Your rod and your staff
have comforted me.
You have set tables before me
in the sight of my enemies.
You have anointed my head with oil.
And my cup gives joy like pure wine.
Your loving kindness and your compassion
have pursued me all the days of my life.
And I will live in the house of the Lord
for the rest of my days!

The Word "Psalm"

In Aramaic the word for psalm is *mazmora,* which is cognate with the Hebrew *mizmor*. Its Semitic root is *zmar*, "to sing," "to chant," "to talk with tones," "to play on a stringed instrument." The Hebrew word for the book of Psalms is *tehillim*, "praises." Our English term and title "Psalms" come from the Greek word *psalmoi*, "songs of praise," by way of the Latin *psalmorum*. Today, as in the past, the psalms function among Jews and Christians as a hymnal for worship and a prayer book for devotion.

In the ancient Near East, shepherds sometimes sang these

psalms and then later poets put them to their lips and gave praise to the God of Israel. Temple singers glorified God with these psalms in the midst of the worshipers. Some psalms represent the prayers of Israel for deliverance from oppressors. Other psalms were songs of joy when Israel triumphed over its enemies.

A Metaphysical Idea—A Biblical Idea

A teacher of biblical metaphysics once told me that every place in the Bible where we read the term "Lord," we need to substitute the word "law." By this, the educator implied that we can drop the name of God—*Yahweh* or Lord—and change it to a metaphysical concept, such as "divine law or principle." As an example, instead of saying, "The Lord is my shepherd," we can say, "Divine Law is my shepherd."

However, during biblical times, interpreting God as Law, Process, Divine Principle, Individual Reality, Divine Consciousness, Infinite Intelligence or even as Love Intelligence would not have appealed to the shepherds, farmers, and common folk of the land. They would not have grasped such abstract terminology. All the above expressions are modern and broadly sophisticated ideas of God.

When the biblical writers referred to their Deity, they portrayed God as a Father, Friend, Savior, King, and Great Shepherd. The modern mind has a difficult time relating to these human, intimate, and rudimentary biblical terms and ideas about God. Yet, if we would look more closely at the biblical notions, we would see their rich and relevant meanings for today's society.

For example, God as *our* Father means all humans are

children of God and not just a few special human beings. All races are offspring of the one Creator[2] whom the Hebrew Scripture calls God and Father. As one rabbi put it, "We have one God and Father of us all so that one person cannot say to another that my father is better than yours."

When we understand God as the creative power of every human being, we come to realize the one resourceful potential in all races of humanity. This example is simple and clear. As we recognize our one spiritual source (God), divisions no longer exist. Usually, we perceive ethnic and racial diversity as separations, but they are merely differentiations. What would this world be like without variety and diversity? Sameness makes everything appear dull. Now let us explore the 23rd psalm keeping in mind what I have written above.

The Verb "To Shepherd"

The first verse of this enchanting song is a powerful affirmation of truth. In Hebrew the text reads a little differently from the Aramaic text: "The Lord is my Shepherd, I shall not want." But in Aramaic it reads: "The Lord shepherds me and I lack nothing at all!" Instead of the noun "shepherd," the Peshitta text uses an action verb "shepherds." This denotes God in the act of shepherding.

The Aramaic verb *raa* not only means "to shepherd" but also "to feed," "to tend," "to herd," "to keep," "to pastor," "to nourish." Metaphorically it signifies "to rule," "to lead," and "to govern." Clearly, the idea is that God guides and nourishes us.

----

[2]In metaphysics we would refer to this phenomenon as the one Creative Principle rather than Creator.

168

The First Affirmation

When we acknowledge and meditate upon this opening verse we declare that God is alive in our hearts and souls. It is a practical and affirmative statement of truth. "The Lord guides me and I lack nothing at all!" When this verse becomes a part of us mentally and emotionally, then that spiritual principle becomes active in our lives. It awakens us to the reality that God is directing us. The key point to remember is that this power gently *guides us* and *does not drive us*. In Aramaic and Hebrew the word guidance speaks of being led and not forcefully driven.

The composer of the song had a deep, abiding conviction that God sees after us exactly as a skilled shepherd cares for his sheep. We understand this principle from an inner realization. As this inner presence shepherds us, we find ourselves walking in paths of goodness and truth.

God is spirit, love, joy, and peace. Therefore, it is spirit and love that direct us on the abundant path which reveals life and peace. We will see as we read the following verses what happens when spiritual forces we call God shepherd us from day to day.

Sheep—Symbol of Dependency

Occasionally, I have encountered misunderstanding from some individuals about the opening phrase of this psalm—"The Lord is my shepherd." When we repeat this line, we declare that we are sheep. But, how can we be compared to sheep?

The problem is that we often think of sheep as dumb animals. We know that they are constantly having to be led about, fed, protected, and cared for like children. This is true.

However, we miss the point if we think this way. Biblically, sheep represent a spiritual principle. Sheep symbolize the principle of dependency upon God.

We ordinarily think of ourselves as self-reliant beings and we usually are. But, let us pause for a moment and think about the ways that we are self-reliant. For instance, did *we* make our bodies grow? Or, did nature make us grow?

Of course, we didn't make our bodies grow. Our natural body functions work with voluntary and involuntary physical energies. Thus, we are totally dependent on so many invisible, involuntary actions of our bodies. Besides these inner physical forces that maintain health and growth, we must also rely on our environment. We depend upon clean air, pure water, nutritious food, and on many other unseen forces and realities that are outside us.

Undoubtedly, we are self-reliant beings but only to a certain extent. We definitely have to rely on many other influences in this life besides ourselves. And, more often than not, we don't even think about these other factors.

According to the gospel of John, Jesus said, "I can do nothing of my self."[3] He relied upon God, who was the invisible source of his being. Jesus as a great master-teacher was a sheep also; that is, like a sheep he was wholly dependent on God to shepherd him. Although we know that Jesus was a self-reliant man, his reliance was based upon an invisible side of himself—the essence of his soul.

Thus, we too have an unseen source, an origin we cannot fully rationalize. In our modern age, we call this source or power by many different names and titles—"God," "Father," "Father-Mother God," "Divine Mind," "Inner Wisdom," "Higher Self,"

---

[3]Jn. 5:30.

170

"Spiritual Forces," "Infinite Loving Intelligence," and so forth and so on.

In reality, we cannot escape the powers of inner forces that continually shepherd us. As for the ancient psalmist, he delighted in the idea of dependence upon God as a guiding light in his life. His heart was truly grateful and thankful. He was not ashamed to acknowledge the power of God in his life.

The Great Shepherd

The great shepherd was the chief shepherd. All other shepherds were answerable to him. He was the overseer for all the flocks and occupied a very important position in the community. The late Near-Eastern theologian Dr. George M. Lamsa says:

> My ancestors for untold generations were sheep raising people. My father and my mother loved and tended sheep. I was raised in a sheep camp. We lived in a tent made of the hair of goats just as Abraham and Isaac did. Like other boys, I was taught and disciplined by the shepherd. Since my father was chief shepherd, I was taught through his wisdom.[4]

For endless generations, sheep raising has been the highest occupation in Arabia, Palestine, and Mesopotamia until the arrival of Western technology in the Near East. Life in these lands changes very slowly. Dr. Lamsa, who thought very highly of this occupation, said: "Sheep raising is an occupation where

---

[4]Lamsa, George M., *The Shepherd of All: The Twenty-third Psalm*, "Foreword" pp. 7–8.

greed, dishonesty, and crookedness are seldom found, and where sharing and hospitality prevail."[5]

A skilled shepherd is vital in the Near East. Without an adept shepherd, the sheep will scatter and become the prey of thieves and every kind of vicious beast. Human beings without spiritual guidance also become victims of false notions, absurd teachings, and crafty human predators. Interestingly, most holy men, prophets, and great leaders in the Bible were shepherds.

A chief shepherd must know how to lead his people as well as their flocks. He has to know the lay of the land, its pastures, hidden wells, the seasons, and where to find the oases. He must be able to fight off wild animals, be willing to heal and dress the sick and wounded sheep and even be willing to give his life for the sheep. And, above all, he must not show partiality toward any particular flock.

The chief shepherd must treat everyone equally. His responsibility was a great one to carry. There is no doubt that his position was unique and crucial. He made sure that the sheep never lacked a thing. We need to understand this principle from an inner realization. It is God who shepherds us. God always guides us into paths of truth and goodness.

But what is God? How does God shepherd us? God is spirit, love, joy, and peace. Therefore, spirit, love, joy, and peace are the inner powers that shepherd us. We never lack when these forces guide us in all we do. We can now better understand the meaning of this first verse: "The LORD shepherds me and I lack nothing at all!" The following verses clearly describe what happens when God shepherds people.

---

[5]Ibid., "The Shepherd," p. 11.

Pastures of Strength

"And in pastures of strength he makes me dwell. He guides me by restful waters. He has restored my life (soul)!" Near Eastern shepherds look for rich, fertile grazing areas where water is ample and grass is plentiful. They especially look for such places near mountains because it is usually cool and shaded. It is also a place where the entire camp may enjoy the richness of the land.

Where there is a bounteous supply, women who milk the sheep have only short distances to walk and perform their daily tasks. Because of the abundance, the chief shepherd also spends his time at the camp. He will be taking care of the sheep, adjusting broken bones, and doctoring the sheep's feet.

"Pastures of strength" are symbolic of harmony, security, and peace. It refers to rich and fertile fields. In the Hebrew Bible, it says "He makes me to lie down in *green* pastures." This also signifies "abundance," as well as the above mentioned symbolic interpretations. In Aramaic the verb *shra* means "to dwell, lodge, stay, reside," "to lie down," and "to rest upon."

Sheep enjoy pastures that are fertile and abound in grazing areas. In this kind of field, sheep do not have to go far at all. They can lie down and eat. This almost effortless form of grazing makes the sheep fatter and more content. When they are well cared for and satisfied, they produce better wool and by-products.

The meaning here is very easy to understand. In this line of the psalm, we affirm that God guides us in fields that strengthen us. We prosper inwardly and outwardly.

Restful Waters

"Restful waters" refer to sweet, clear, slow-running water. When water moves too swiftly for sheep, then they cannot drink. If this is the case, the shepherd will build small nooks near the edges of the stream to make it easier for his flocks to drink. Also sheep will not drink still, stagnant water. Their shepherd always tests the water before they drink.

Sweet, restful, refreshing water represents truth and enlightenment. In the Near East, when one dreams of clear waters, it means one is about to receive truth and understanding. However, when a Near Easterner dreams of dark and murky waters, it signifies trouble and difficult times ahead.

In the ancient Near Eastern lands, water was scarce and very precious. (Today, modern Western technology is solving many water problems for the Near East.) Biblical writers symbolize truth by referring to it as water. For them, truth was as precious as water; without it we cannot live.

When Easterners are dying of thirst, they often say, "My life (soul) has left me." But, when someone is kind enough to give and share water with these thirsty travelers, one usually hears a grateful saying such as, "You have restored my life (soul)!" Or one may also hear, "You have saved my life!"

Also, at times, some sheep may stray or thieves may carry them off, then the shepherd must find the ones who have gone astray, or bargain with those who have stolen them. The shepherd must restore these sheep to the flock.

Again, we affirm that God guides us to clear water so that we may drink and not perish. Spiritual enlightenment restores our souls (life) and shines in our hearts and minds. Truth or enlightenment is like clear water; it refreshes and restores clarity and life to us all.

174

Paths of Justice

"And upon pathways of justice, he leads me. Because of your reputation, even if I walk through the valleys of the shadows of death, I fear no danger. Because You are with me."

The chief shepherd knows all the safe pathways upon which to guide his flocks. He must be careful not to take short cuts through rocky and treacherous paths. His sheep might fall and break their legs.

Also he will not lead them through vineyards or wheatfields because the landowners might seize and kill them. After all, the shepherd's name (reputation) is at stake. He will lose his good name as a competent shepherd if he does not skillfully lead the sheep who are in his care.

Metaphysically, "the chief shepherd" refers to the spirit of truth that guides us into paths of justice. This spiritual power counsels our hearts when we acknowledge its presence in our lives. God's presence helps us to choose paths that are not stony or dangerous. But if we must travel a hazardous path, God is with us.

Perilous Paths

"The valleys of the shadows of death" are winding paths between mountains where dark shadows may obscure many perils for the travelers. Bandits and thieves usually hide in dens and caves. Leading sheep through these valleys is an extremely tense and dangerous experience. In a Jewish commentary published in London by Soncino Press LTD, the rabbinical author tells us the following about the dangers of tending sheep:

The Hebrew, however, signifies only "deep gloom," and the Psalmist is not thinking of his departure from the world. Being himself a shepherd, he recalls a familiar experience in his occupation, and figuratively compares it with God's protection of him. The manner of tending sheep in the East is very different from that practiced among ourselves, and supplies many illustrations to the poetry and the parables of Holy Writ. The sheep districts consist of wide-open wolds or downs, reft here and there by deep ravines, in whose sides lurk many a wild beast, the enemy of the flocks. He [the shepherd] likewise has sometimes to pass through dark ways with the possibility of being suddenly attacked by lurking foes.[6]

It is often said in the Near East that a person may be "under the shadow of death." This signifies that the individual's life is in danger. He could be killed at any moment. Only God's presence, which biblical authors have symbolized as light, can brighten one's path, dispelling fears (shadows).

Those who know God's guiding presence fear no evildoer or calamity. Fear has a difficult time gripping and clutching our hearts as we continue to realize and rest in the assuring presence of God. We may sense danger all around us but terror cannot take hold of us. God is with us!

The Rod and Staff

"Your rod and your staff have comforted me" refers to discipline and protection. Near Eastern shepherds carry rods and

---

[6]The Rev. Dr. A. Cohen, *The Psalms*, "The Divine Shepherd," p. 68.

staffs. They use their rods to direct the sheep and the staffs become weapons to protect them from wild animals, snakes, and thieves.

Generally, the shepherd who has been appointed to care for the lambs of the flock carries a tender rod (a branch of a tree or from a bush) and gently taps the lambs on their backs while guiding them. Sheep feel comforted by the guiding rod and protecting staff of their shepherd. Figuratively, the rod and the staff represent spiritual discipline and true teaching which protect us from anything that may be false or harmful.

Prosperity

"You have set tables before me in the sight of my enemies. You have anointed my head with oil. And my cup gives joy like pure wine."

A blest and prosperous table is one that has abundant food and stacks of bread piled high for everyone to see, including one's enemies. A bounteous table that has plenty of food speaks well of the family's reputation, especially the head of the household. It is difficult to describe just how famous a family may become when its table is so plentiful with food.

There is nothing more embarrassing to an enemy than to discover that the table of a hated individual or family has become so very generous and prosperous. Now the enemy cannot say anything bad. Prosperity has negated the harmful gossip. Figuratively, when God "sets our table" it means that God prospers us. Prosperity comes in spite of those who may envy us and wish us misfortune.

Near Easterners often use butter, olive oil, and wine for medicine as well as for food. They anoint their heads with olive oil and also use it on chapped hands and feet. These items are very expensive. Therefore when they own these things, they consider themselves living a life of luxury.

When butter and olive oil are scarce, they use them sparingly, mostly for food and for emergency medicine only. The cup that gives great joy represents more than ample supply of food and drink. All these particular phrases of the psalm refer to prosperity. The bounteous table, the anointing oil, and the cup that enlivens one represent great wealth and health.

Compassion and Loving Kindness

"Your loving kindness and your compassion have pursued (literally: chased and persecuted) me all the days of my life. And I shall live in the house of the Lord for the rest of my days." Sheep-raising, migrating tribes are always in search of grass and water. They often have to settle in places where the people are unfriendly or hostile to them. They pray for God to favor them, that is, through his loving kindness may they find peace and acceptance while they live among strangers and unfriendly tribes.

The psalmist sings of God's continual grace (loving kindness) and compassion wherever he goes throughout his lifetime. God had granted him favor and mercy among strangers everywhere. The Semitic term *radpoon* means "to chase down," "to hunt," "to pursue," and "to persecute." In other words, God's compassion and loving kindness were relentless in their pursuit of the psalmist. They, literally, hounded him all the days of his life.

The final shepherding act of God is to lead all humanity home to the temple (house) of truth, love, and peace. It is the destiny of every human being to rest and live in the loving presence of God, i.e., Infinite Love, Joy, and Wholeness. "And I shall live in the house of the Lord forever."

26

Repent—An About Face

What does it mean "to repent?" Does it simply mean "to feel sorry?" Contrary to the popular belief about this Semitic word, it has a clear, concise meaning. Hebrew prophets, John the Baptist, Jesus, and his apostles continually admonished their people to repent.

Translators usually render two basic Aramaic root words for "repent" and they are *pna* and *tob*. The first term, *pna*, means "to turn, to turn toward, to turn back, to return, to be restored, given back and returned to the owner." The second word, *tob*, means "to return, come again, to flow back, and to turn to God." Both of these root terms may be paraphrased as "doing an about face."

Turning Away / Turning Toward

In our popular religious use of the word "repent," we often think of turning from or turning away, but the Semitic use of this term is more positive. The emphasis in Aramaic and Hebrew carries the idea of "turning toward" rather than just "turning away or from" something. Frequently, in our attempts to resist darkness or temptation, we find ourselves being drawn into it. But the idea here is to turn toward something positive. For example, if we are in a dark tunnel and then see a light in the darkness, we naturally will turn to the light and move in its direction. Thus, when we turn to the Source—God—we need

180

not concern ourselves with turning away from something that is harmful. To discover our Source is to find the pure fountain of joy, love, peace, and profound fulfillment. True repentance means we are totally occupied in turning toward the light.

Repentance

The Aramaic noun for "repentance" is *tyawootha* and in Hebrew *teshuvah*. Its Hebrew root is *shuvu* or *shuwu* and it also means "to return." The idea or concept behind "repentance" is that "one must return to God and the covenant." According to widely attested Jewish sources, "Returning to God, His covenant and the practice of good works bring salvation." In the gospels, the idea of a true turning to God is characterized by the practice of good deeds which go beyond good intentions.

The Hebrew text of the book of psalms reads: "Be still and know that I am God."[1] The Aramaic text literally reads: "Repent and know that I am God." I translate the phrase as, "Turn to me and know that I am God." In the opening verses of this same psalm the writer declares: "Our God is our place of relief and strength, and our protector in times of distress. You have always been with us. On account of this, we will not fear when the earth quakes and the mountains are shaken into the depths of the sea."[2]

We can truly know that place in God where there is relief and strength when we sincerely turn to God—that is, turn to the truth of our Being. For knowing God is greater than knowing a

---

[1] Ps. 46:10 KJV

[2] Ps. 46:1-2, Aramaic Peshitta text.

concept about God. This means that there must be an about-face, a realization of our spiritual origin. We must actually know who we are and what we are. Therefore, knowing God reveals the truth about us.

Realization

We come to a realization of God by turning to the original context of our Being. When we are constantly seeing ourselves and others outside of the context of God, we see a distorted picture. Merely turning away from seeing things and people negatively does not give us the full impetus that we need. But by turning to God, the only Self and Source of life, we then see life clearly and positively. Living is joyful when seen totally in the context of God. We do not have to fight or deny so-called "evil." We simply turn to the Source and know that the only true "I" is God. God is Being and Being is God.

Again, let us look at Psalms 46:10. This time I am going to amplify verse 10 of the psalm with meanings derived from the Aramaic words. "Be restored, [turn back, flow back to the Source] and know that I am God—infinite love, peace, joy and assurance."

Summary

So what does all this mean? It means that as we do an about-face in our present style of living and turn toward the Source of our Being, we uncover the truth about ourselves. We discover a joyful, loving life style that is completely free of any distorted picture of ourselves and of life. We then truly find that

182

our Source is God, our place of relief and strength for the rest of our lives.

27

The Power of Knowing

According to John's gospel, Jesus says: "And you will *know* the truth, and that very truth will set you free."[1] Interestingly, the teacher from Galilee *did not say*, "And you will *believe* the truth and that very truth will set you free." The gospel writer has Jesus place his emphasis on the word "*know*." This term "know" in the Semitic languages of Aramaic and Hebrew differs from our English word "know." The richness of this Semitic term has a far wider range and greater scope than in English.

Before I begin describing the extent of this Semitic word "know" there is another verse of scripture for us to consider. In the Hebrew Bible, the psalmist says: "*Be still* and *know* that I am God."[2] But, in the Aramaic text this same verse reads as: "*Turn to me* and *know* that I am God."

What it Means "To Know"

One usually has to translate the Semitic verb *y-d* as "*to know*." Our English equivalent for this verb does not fully convey the Semitic, Near Eastern idea behind the verb. The ancient biblical idea of *knowledge* is not basically or fundamentally grounded in the intellect. Knowledge, according to Semitic thinking, is not just a mental and intellectual activity. For Near

---

[1] Jn. 8:32, Aramaic Peshitta text.

[2] Ps. 46:10, KJV.

Easterners *knowing* is more experiential.

They believe that *knowing* is rooted in the emotions, and not just in the mind. For example, the author of Genesis 4:1 tells us: "So Adam *knew* Eve his wife and she conceived and gave birth to Cain." Thus, *knowing* also refers to bodily, physical intimacy. In both languages, Aramaic and Hebrew, *knowing* encompasses human qualities such as care, understanding, communication, relatedness, and commonality. It is something we *feel* and not just something we know mentally.

For instance, saying we *know God* does not mean we can *explain* God. We meet this identical challenge when attempting to explain the meaning of the word "love." Certainly, we can *know* love—that is, we can *feel* and *apprehend* love—but can we define what love really is?

East Versus West

In our Western society it seems we have split ourselves into intellect and feeling. For us the intellect reigns supreme and our emotions usually have to play a subordinate role. But the truth is that emotions and intellect belong together because both comprise a true sense of *knowing*. Knowledge is important. But, are we merely retaining information or are we really making a connection with what or with whom we know?

When our knowing is deeply rooted in the sacred channels of our emotions, we become thoroughly connected with our humanity and that of others also. But when our knowing is disconnected from our souls and bodies, we easily create coldness, indifference, alienation, and estrangement. Thus, genuine *knowing,* which originates from our emotional body-self and not just from our intellect, generates warmth and life. It

185

keeps us in harmony with ourselves mentally and emotionally.

A Neurological Experience

Knowing is a neurological experience. It is not just our brain or head that knows something. Our bodies also know. Have you not ever listened to a very prolonged speech that merely presented facts and figures? Or, have you ever listened to a speaker whose presentation was extremely dry? Something happens to our bodies.

Generally, our bodies respond by becoming tired, restless, or perhaps even numb. The information we are hearing is reaching our intellects only. Thus, when our minds reach an overload of accumulated information, our bodies will react, demanding recreation and movement.

Biblical writers understood the meaning of *knowing*. It is truly neurological. They did not understand it as "neurological" but as a total bodily experience. It is a comprehensive experience—spirit, soul, and body. Thus, "You shall know the truth," means "realizing truth as vital energy that nourishes every particle of our being."

Knowing God

Let us recall the psalm that says: "Be still and *know* that I am God." Therefore, we come to know God not just as an idea for the intellect but as a living presence that is felt in the entire nervous system. When this happens, every cell in our bodies senses this living essence we call God.

Today, religious advocates constantly admonish their

listeners "to believe." However, both verses of scripture, Psalm 46:10 and John 8:32, emphasize "knowing" and not "believing." The psalmist tells us to become still so that we may know God. Actually, it is easier to believe or not believe in someone after we come to know that individual. How can one trust another without knowing him or her first? Having confidence in a someone presents no problem when we come to know that person..

When we quiet our hearts and minds, we can know God. And as we turn to this invisible presence we call God we come into a realization of joy, health, and freedom. "And you will *know* the truth and that very truth will set you free."

28

Divine Protection

"He who dwelleth in the secret place of the most High shall abide under the shadow of the Almighty. . . For he shall give his angels charge over thee, to keep thee in all thy ways.[1]

Secret Place

The Aramaic word for "secret place" is *sitara*, which also means " a sure, safe, and protected place." In those very ancient days, kings and princes had secret places in which to hide themselves from their enemies. These special places were the strongest and most secure in their palaces, cities or towns. A similar meaning is intended by the psalmist except that the secret place of the most High to which he refers is the Holy Spirit—divine consciousness. This divine place is open to all who wish to enter. It is called a "secret place" because it is hidden from human eyes and understanding. It is not a physical location but a state of Being.

Dwelling

The term "dwell" is from the Aramaic *yateb* and means "to repose" or "to sit down." The idea implies a state of mind in

---

[1]Ps. 91:1, 11 KJV.

which one is in total repose, completely at rest, and settled in an awareness of God's presence. This "God consciousness" means one's sense of awareness is captivated by love, peace, and joy which is God's presence. These very things are the spiritual principles and values in life.

In order "to dwell in the secret place of the most High" one must cease from laborious efforts to find and secure a safe place in this world. There is none. One simply needs to realize the truth of God's goodness for him/herself right now and rest in that assurance. This secret place lies within the individual.

Shadow

"Shadow," figuratively speaking, also signifies protection. In the Near East when a king or ruler is kind and good to his subjects, the people often speak of him in such terms as "We are under a good shadow," meaning "We are well protected."

(There are also other instances in the Hebrew Scripture where the writers use the term "shadow" to depict fear and uncertainty, as in the 23rd psalm. Here it refers to the "valley of the *shadow* of death.") Again, the psalmist says to us that he who has settled for living truth in his life, and not just a doctrine of truth, will abide under the protection of the most High. And in verse 11 the psalmist tells us that God will "give his angels charge over you and keep you in all your ways."

Angels

The term "angels" in Aramaic means "messengers." Metaphorically it refers to "God's counsel, presence, or thoughts." Thus the phrase "for he shall give his angels charge over you," denotes that God, who is love, will guide you and guard you in all your ways. When good counsel and understanding guide us, we naturally have right action and therefore live in protection. Inappropriate thoughts lead us into improper action from which we will suffer.

Let us amplify the first part of this psalm based on the meanings of the Aramaic words. "He who rests in the secure, hidden place of the most High shall live under the protection of the Almighty." As we continually make our home in God, and as we constantly live in the Spirit—the spirit of truth and love—we find ourselves protected wherever we are. The only sure and secure place to live is in a God centered life in the spirit.

29

Angels

Malakha, in Aramaic, usually translates into English as
"angel." Our English word "angel" comes from the Greek
language, *angelos. Malakha* means "messenger," "sent one."
Thus, an angel simply means "a sent one." However, this term
has other nuances.

When Scripture says "The angel of the Lord (Yahweh)
appeared," it means God's messenger— one who carries God's
message—is appearing in a dream or vision. (So many biblical
narratives tell of angelic appearances.) Hence, "angels" in the
Bible also mean God's ideas or thoughts. One has to determine
its meaning by understanding the biblical context.

Spiritual ideas (angels) may come in dreams, night visions
or even in daydreams. However they may appear, one must be
in a modified state of awareness. Usually only the person
receiving the vision sees the angel and hears the message.

A Metaphysical Meaning

Metaphysically, an angel is a heavenly thought form. It is an
inspired perception. Many biblical episodes about angelic
visitations were in reality God's presence advising and guiding
the individual receiving the revelation. Recipients of angelic
visitations were in altered states of consciousness. They could
now receive the inspired thoughts of God.

We are going to examine some biblical verses about angels.

The reader must realize that the Bible treats the subject of angels extensively. In this chapter we will only mention a few scriptural passages that readers may have misunderstood.

Angels: A Flame of Fire

Psalm 104:4 reads: "...who [God] makes his angels spirits, his ministers a flame of fire." This psalm refers to God's greatness and his wondrous creations. "Angels" represent God's counsel. "Spirit" in this passage denotes everywhere. The psalmist tells us that God's message and counsel are universal and everywhere. An Aramaic expression that is still in use today is: "He is like a flame of fire." This means that the individual is a genius and speedy in his actions. In this passage, the psalm reveals that God's thoughts (angels) are universal, powerful, and swift like fire. They are his ministers, instantaneously carrying his word everywhere.

Entertaining Angels

In the letter to the Hebrews, the author admonishes the people to show hospitality to strangers, for one never knows who the stranger might be. They could even be "angels." "And forget not hospitality toward strangers for thereby some were worthy to entertain angels unaware"[1] "Angels" in this scripture can mean a prophet, minister, or a man of God.

In general, Easterners are well-known for their hospitality toward strangers and travelers. Very often when strangers arrive

---

[1]Heb. 13:2, Aramaic Peshitta text, Lamsa translation.

192

in a town, they will receive invitations to stay at the homes of different families. People freely share their food and provide water so that the guests may wash their feet. Usually visitors (strangers) do not reveal their identity until they feel truly welcomed. A host may be surprised to discover that the unexpected stranger may be a nobleman or a prophet.

Respect to the Angels

Paul writes a curious admonition in his letter to the Corinthians. This passage of scripture is difficult for many readers to understand. "For this cause ought the woman to have power on her head because of the angels.[2] However, the Eastern Aramaic text reads differently. "Because of this the woman ought to have the right to cover her head out of respect to the angels." (Errico translation.

To understand this passage, we need to know the Eastern custom that lies behind it. Near Easterners believe that when they pray, angels are present to carry their supplications before God's throne. But saintly, pious, and charitable men and women are also addressed as "angels of God." In this verse the term "angels" means "holy (or pious) men."

Paul grew up in Judaism and was a faithful observer of Mosaic ordinances. He also had learned many laws and doctrines at the school in Jerusalem. Thus, in admonishing the women of the Corinthian Church, he refers to a Jewish religious custom, as well as to a Near Eastern social code. The unwritten social code was for women to cover their faces (heads) in the presence of holy men (angels) not as a sign of fear, but out of

---

[2]1 Cor. 11:10, KJV.

respect, dignity, and reverence.

Interestingly, Jesus ignored all man-made Jewish ordinances and many of the social customs of his day. He knew that men and women were the image and likeness of God. He said nothing about women covering their heads. Jesus was actually notorious for ignoring many cultural ideas.

In the last book of the New Testament, a messenger had commanded John on the isle of Patmos to write to the seven angels of the seven Asia Minor churches. (See Revelation 2:1, 8, 12, and 18.) Here, in these verses, the term "angels" refers to the appointed head of that particular church to whom John wrote. Angelic, heavenly beings would not need to have a letter written to them. But the head minister or pastor would need the letter of admonition.

Angels and Dreams

The appearances of angels in the Bible generally take place in a dream state. For example, when Scripture says: "And the angel of the Lord (Yahweh) appeared to him (Moses) in a flame of fire out of the midst of the bush. . . ." This means Moses was receiving a vision. The word "appeared," *eth-gli*, also implies "to come through or by revelation." Divine communications were commonly imparted through visions and dreams. There is a passage in the book of Job that says this very clearly. "For God speaks once. He does not speak a second time. In a dream, in a vision of the night, when deep sleep falls upon men, while slumbering upon the bed. Then he opens the ears of men, and humbles them according to their rebelliousness."[3]

---

[3]Job 33:14-16, Aramaic Peshitta text, Lamsa translation.

30

Spiritual Leadership

"And there shall come forth a rod out of the stem of Jesse, and a branch shall grow out of his roots. And the spirit of the Lord (Yahweh) shall rest upon him, the spirit of wisdom and understanding, the spirit of counsel and might, the spirit of knowledge and of the fear [reverence] of the Lord. And he shall make him of quick understanding in the fear [reverence] of the Lord. And he shall not judge after the sight of his eyes, neither reprove after the hearing of his ears. But with righteousness shall he judge the poor, and reprove with equity for the meek of the earth. And he shall smite the earth with the rod of his mouth, and with the breath of his lips shall he slay the wicked."[1]

The Coming Leader

This prophecy belongs to the reign of King Ahaz or, according to others, to the latter days of Isaiah's life. Isaiah predicted that an anointed leader (the Messiah) was to demonstrate the same attributes as King David who once ruled Israel. David symbolizes power, strength of character, and obedience to God. This prophet-statesman, Isaiah, employs Semitic figures of speech to describe the Messiah's power and authority and the coming messianic age.

---

[1]Isa. 11:1-4, KJV.

Figures of Speech

Let us examine some of the terms that the prophet uses. "Stem of Jesse" refers to the family of Jesse, the father of King David. "Rod" and "branch" denote an heir—a natural-born heir or a spiritual heir. He mentions seven spirits: The spirit of the Lord, of wisdom, understanding, counsel, might, knowledge, and reverence. The number seven always signifies "fullness" or "completion." Seven spirits represent the fullness of God's presence. This fullness speaks of a new world order where wisdom, justice, and peace reign supreme.

These qualities that distinguish an ideal spiritual leader are categorized in three directions. They relate to the leader's intellectual, administrative, and spiritual attributes. "Wisdom and understanding" relate to the intellect. His governmental ability, a sense of true justice (judgment), manifests in "counsel and might." Spirituality manifests in "knowledge and reverence of the Lord"

A Metaphysical Meaning

Metaphysically, it means that only when human beings are under the influence of God's spirit will they conquer injustices and false leadership. True judgment (justice) relies not on what the ears may hear or what the eyes may see. It relies on the spirit of truth (God) that is neither personal nor impersonal. Thus, truth and judgment are transpersonal and transcendent.

A Spiritual Awareness

A spiritual consciousness reproves the world's violence, injustices, greed, and oppression. An enlightened heart and mind dispel all false and deceptive forms of thinking. Love, peace, justice, and truth must begin in every individual internally before world peace can show itself outwardly.

Racism, prejudice, and fear all come from within an individual. Therefore, we must receive healing within our beings. Legislation can only temporarily stem the tide of violence. The spirit of wisdom, understanding, counsel, strength, knowledge and reverence for God heal us from within. God is life itself. When we respect God, we respect life in all its forms. Violence has no place in this spiritual economy.

The harsh and violent sounding Semitic expressions such as "Smite the earth with the rod of his mouth and the breath of his lips" and "slay the wicked" are metaphors. These metaphors depict a nonviolent approach to ruling. How could anyone fight with a rod in the mouth or destroy with the breath of the lips? All these Semitic expressions describe a spiritual teaching that disciplines and corrects all inequities including all people who practice injustice.

197

31

Rooha—Spirit

The Semitic term *rooha* , "spirit," can be troublesome to translate into English. It has so many different meanings. Anyone wanting to translate this word *rooha* must consider its context so that one may determine its significance.

Assyrians and Chaldeans who still speak Aramaic today use this word "spirit" to carry various ideas and meanings. For example, when these people talk about a dynamic, charismatic speaker, they say: "he or she has *rooha* ." This means that the speaker's personality and characteristics are powerful, brilliant, and extremely persuasive. They also use the word *rooha* to describe someone with a very hot temper. Let us now explore the biblical use of *rooha* , "spirit."

Spirit and Sickness

There is a story in the gospel of Luke that narrates a particular healing that a woman received under Jesus' ministry. Luke records the illness as a "spirit of infirmity." "And behold, there was a woman which had a spirit of infirmity eighteen years, and was bowed together, and could in no wise lift up herself."[1] The Aramaic text reads: "There was a woman who was present and she had been afflicted with rheumatism for eighteen years. She was bent over and never was able to

---

[1]Lk. 13:11, KJV.

198

straighten up in any way."[2] Jesus healed this woman of her long-term crippling rheumatoid arthritis. In those days, people did not have a scientific understanding of diseases so they used the word "spirit" to describe them.

Unclean Spirit

According to many gospel narratives, Jesus cast out "unclean spirits." These different scriptural passages usually refer to various mental and emotional illnesses. Semitic people did not have medical terms to describe illnesses. New Testament writers employed the term "spirit," *rooha ,* to indicate all kinds of physical, emotional, and mental disturbances.

Jesus healed Mary of Magdala who had seven unclean spirits. This does not mean that seven entities possessed her. "Seven" is typically Semitic and connotes completeness. An extremely bad and harmful conduct had dominated Mary of Magdala completely. Jesus cleansed her of these bad habits. Her demeanor and behavior changed totally. She found healing through Jesus' ministry.

Paul, the apostle, also admonished Christian converts to cleanse themselves from all "filthiness of spirit." How can "spirit" be filthy? "Filthiness of spirit" is an Aramaic idiom. We may also translate this Aramaic phrase as "Cleanse yourself from all unwholesome inclinations." Paul wanted the followers of Jesus to be mindful of harmful, corrupt desires. So, the term "spirit," *rooha*, also means an "inclination."

---

[2]Aramaic Peshitta text.

Other Meanings

In many passages "Spirit" indicates radiation, vibration, influence, inspiration, universal, and at least a dozen more meanings. We determine the sense of the word through context. For example "evil spirit" can denote a bad demeanor or jealousy. "And it came to pass on the morrow, that the evil spirit from God came upon Saul, and he prophesied in the midst of the house. Then David played with his hand [the harp], as at other times. And there was a javelin in Saul's hand. And Saul cast the javelin; for he said, I will smite David even to the wall with it. And David avoided out of his presence twice."[3]

Did God send an evil spirit upon Saul? To answer this question we must consider the cultural and religious beliefs of that time. During this period of Israel's history, people had no concept of a devil—Satan—as we do today. (This notion came into existence during the Jewish captivity in Babylon.)[4] The Hebrews believed that everything happened with God's permission. These people attributed all events, good or bad, to God.

David had just slain Goliath and now the Israelite women of the court were praising David more than Saul, their own King. Their song of praise said that Saul had slain by the thousands but David by the tens of thousands. In reality David had only slain one man, Goliath. This is what provoked King Saul. His demeanor changed and he became jealous of David.

The historical writer of 1 Samuel uses the women's song as

---

[3]1 Sam. 18:10-11, KJV.

[4]See Rocco A. Errico, *Let There Be Light: The Seven Keys,* "Satan" pp. 40-41, "The Term Devil" p. 43, and "Lucifer" pp. 137-139, 1994.

the provocation for Saul's jealousy. But there was more to it than just the song. It is what the song represents—David receiving greater fame than Saul. There were strong political implications in the song.

"And he prophesied in the midst of the house" means that Saul called his family together and started making predictions that David was going to be a rival. "House" refers to the family. David was to rival Saul's sons. Saul could see what was coming politically so he decided to kill David. After all, King Saul was interested in his own dynasty.

God does not send evil spirits. We create them ourselves through our own reaction to circumstances. We bring on our own jealousies and resentments. This comes about because we do not understand the truth concerning ourselves. It is difficult to perceive life in its true spiritual context.

God's Spirit as Meekness

"Then he answered and spake unto me saying, This is the word of the Lord unto Zerubbabel, saying, Not by might, nor by power, but by my spirit, saith the Lord of hosts."[5] "My spirit" means God's presence and influence. Zechariah, the prophet, declares to Zerubbabel, Israel's leader, that it is not by armed forces ("might") nor by any human power that the remnant of Israel is to conquer. Zerubbabel must learn to rely on the greatest defense in the world, the power of meekness. "Spirit," *rooha* , in this verse means "meekness." It is the only power that can save humankind. It was the only power that could establish the second commonwealth of Israel. Jesus said, "Delighted are

---

[5]Zech. 4:6, KJV.

the meek for they shall inherit the earth."[6]

Spirit Means Power

"And it shall come to pass afterward, that I will pour out my spirit upon all flesh. Your sons and your daughters shall prophesy, your old men shall dream dreams, your young men shall see visions."[7] "I will pour out my spirit upon all flesh" means that God will give the common people abundant power so that they may utter prophecies. God will grant them gifts of insight. On the day of Pentecost, this prediction was fulfilled. Simon Peter stood up and repeated Joel's prophecy. (See Acts 2:1-21.) Both Joel and Simon Peter understood that it would take men and women of spiritual vision to bring about a change in the world. Peace on earth can only come through human beings and in no other way. God will not interfere or intervene. God works through men and women. Besides the gifts of the spirit of God, there are also the fruits of the spirit. These spiritual fruits are love, joy, meekness, and peace. It takes both spiritual insight and spiritual attributes for humanity to reveal harmony on earth.

Rooha—God

Jesus said in Aramaic: "*Alaha ruhow*," in English, "God is spirit." God is the finest essence in the world. God's spirit is

---

[6]Mt. 5:5, Aramaic Peshitta text.

[7]Joel 2:28, KJV.

universal—everywhere. Jesus brought full understanding to the worship of God. He knew that true worshipers need not be confined to any temple, synagogue, church, mosque, or any particular location. The Christ understood that the whole universe vibrated with the very presence of God. Divine, loving intelligence is everywhere. One cannot contain God as a vessel contains water because God is spirit. The Spirit of God is through everything. We live and move and have our being in God—*rooha*, "spirit." "For in him [God] we live and move and have our being, as some of your own wise men have said, For we are his kindred."[8]

Spirit is the opposite of matter in the sense that matter is ephemeral, measurable, and changeable. It is subject to space and time. Spirit is eternal, immeasurable, changeless, and beyond space and time. We call God the eternal Spirit because spirit is everlasting and transcends all known laws of nature.

Spirit and matter appear to be antagonistic but are actually complementary. Spirit can manifest itself in any form or manner. Spirit is of one substance, essence, and God is that very substance.

---

[8]Acts 17:28, Aramaic Peshitta text, Lamsa translation.

32

Prosperity

Did Jesus, the apostles, and the prophets ever teach prosperity? Yes, they did teach about prosperity in one form or another. Moses and most of the Hebrew prophets taught Israel that if they as a nation would obey the laws of Yahweh, their God, they would prosper. Their lands would be fruitful, their harvests abundant, justice would be established among them, and their families would prosper. If Israel disobeyed, then there would be no prosperity.

"Believe in the Lord (Yahweh) your God, so will ye be established. Believe his prophets and so will ye prosper."[1] "And if you will listen diligently to the voice of the Lord (Yahweh) your God, to observe and to do all his commandments which I commanded you this day the Lord your God will set you on high above all nations of the earth.. . . The Lord will open to you his good storehouse, the heavens, to give you rain for your land in its season. And he will bless all the works of your hands. You will lend to many nations but you will not borrow. You will rule over many nations, but they will not rule over you."[2] Israel, as a nation, was to know material prosperity through its spiritual enlightenment. Moses established a theocratic government based on the laws he instituted. He proclaimed liberty and prosperity throughout the land for the Hebrews.

---

[1]2 Chron. 20:20, KJV.

[2]Dt. 28:1-12, Aramaic Peshitta text.

The Foundation of Prosperity

In the New Testament, John, the Presbyter, in his third general epistle, prays for prosperity. He taught that worldly gain, when established on spiritual principles, will not have any harmful repercussion. He says: "Our beloved, I pray for you that in all things you may prosper and that you may be in good health, even as your life (soul) prospers."[3]

John realized that material prosperity comes from a prospering soul. The word "soul" here means "life." Our well being and prosperity depend on how we lives our lives. Interestingly, the original meaning of the word "wealth" is "well-being" and not just the narrow significance of "acquired material goods."

As an aside, the word "prosper" in Aramaic is *selakh*, which also has four other meanings. It means "to flourish," "to prosper," "to be successful," "to be highly honored," and "to have a splitting headache." Therefore, when one prospers, one must be wise and full of divine counsel so that prosperity does not become "a splitting headache."

Other Examples of Prosperity

Joseph's story in the book of Genesis is a good example of prosperity. Not only did Joseph prosper but in the end of the narrative his entire family prospered. Also, during the famine many peoples from the land of Canaan prospered. Joseph from his boyhood had been disciplined and schooled in the spiritual wisdom of his great-grandfather, Abraham.

He had implicit faith in the God of his fathers. Although

---

[3] 3 Jn. 1:2, Aramaic Peshitta text.

Joseph passed through many troubles and nearly lost his life, he flourished. Israel, (Jacob) his father, says of Joseph: "Joseph is a disciplined son, an educated son; a fruitful bough by a spring, whose branches run over the wall."[4]

Malachi, a Hebrew prophet, encouraged Israel to build Yahweh's temple and to bring in their tithes. "Bring all the tithes into my storehouse that there may be food in my house; and prove me now in this, says the Lord Almighty; and I will open the windows of heaven for you and pour blessings for you until you will say, It is enough! [Literally, 'say when']"[5]

Over Concern

Two thousand years ago Jesus instructed his disciples not to be overly concerned with material gains. "Therefore do not be anxious or say, What will we eat, or what will we drink, or with what will we be clothed? For the people of the world look for these things. Your Father who is in heaven knows that all of these things are also necessary for you. But first, you look for God's sovereign counsel (kingdom) and his goodness, and all these things will abundantly be given to you."[6]

"Kingdom" in Aramaic refers to "sovereignty" and "counsel." God's sovereign counsel is joy, peace, love, and harmony. Therefore, when we realize these genuine qualities in our lives, success and prosperity will flourish in an environment of joy, health, and abundant grace.

---

[4]Gen. 49:22, Aramaic Peshitta text. See also verses 23-26.

[5]Mal. 3:10, Aramaic Peshitta text.

[6]Mt. 6:31-33, Aramaic Peshitta text.

An Abundant Life

According to the book of Genesis, humankind has been given dominion over all God's creation. We are endowed with spiritual powers to create new things that enrich daily living. Humanity has the power to transform the earth into a paradise. In reality human beings have unlimited wisdom and spiritual understanding. We are capable of prospering in all things without pain and suffering. Jesus never taught poverty as a way of life. John reports Jesus saying: "I have come that they might have life and that they might have it in a more excellent way."[7]

---

[7]Jn. 10:10, Aramaic Peshitta text.

33

Healing

"A man was there who had been sick for thirty-eight years. Jesus saw this man lying down, and he knew that he had been waiting for a long time. So he said to him: Are you willing to be healed?"[1] Jesus was ever aware of God's healing forces that were active all the time. His consciousness knew nothing but God's restorative powers, wholeness, and perfection. This prophet from Galilee emanated and radiated a natural flow of life's healing forces wherever he went.

The Aramaic Meaning of Healing

In the gospel of John the author used the Aramaic word *hlm* for our English word "heal." This Aramaic verb means "to heal," "to be healthy," "to make whole," "to be sound," "to cure," "to restore," "to integrate," and "to balance." All nature has within itself an integrating and balancing healing energy. This energy channels itself into and through every living thing. There is healing power in a blade of grass, in a tree, and in animal life. Health and perfection are natural to growth and development. Sickness and imperfection are not authentic. They are unnatural and contrary to the law of God. Jesus had a deep faith and a clear understanding in the power of God to heal and make one whole.

---

[1] Jn. 5:5-6 Aramaic Peshitta text.

Healing in the Human Body

These same healing forces that work in nature are also inherent and constantly at work in the human family. From birth to death, these energies are repairing the physical body, building new cells, and eliminating old ones. Healing energies are constantly alert to any emergency that may arise in the human body.

But we know that the mind controls the physical form. So when one's mind is clear, the whole body is well and healthy. However, when the mind becomes obscured, confusion and illness begin to reign in the body. Jesus said: "The lamp of the body is the eye. If, then, your eye is simple, your entire body is lighted. But if your eye is bad, your entire body will be dark. If, then, the light that is in you is dark, how much more will be your darkness!"[2]

The term "eye" in this verse of scripture refers to the "mind." Although the eye is the physical component through which vision is received, vision also comes through one's mind. There are times when we cannot see, hear, or understand, not because of the impairment of our senses. It is because the mind has become clouded with fears, worries, and misunderstandings. The eye becomes dark or, as Jesus said, "bad" or "diseased."

Many illnesses are manifestations of invalid thinking. Interestingly, the term "sickness" in Aramaic actually means "weakness." Near Eastern people had no idea about germs or bacteria. When they didn't feel well, they would simply say that they felt "weak."

---

[2]Mt. 6:22-23, Aramaic Peshitta text.

Descendants of the Ancient Assyrians

Assyrian people who lived in the Northern mountain vastness of Iraq, most of whom could not read or write, kept ancient biblical customs and manners. Their priests and scribes, who were few, were the only ones who could read and write. People were born, married, and died without anyone making records of their lives nor did they care to have anything recorded. Weeks, months, and years simply flew by without any changes in their way of life or thinking. Dr. Lamsa, the late Assyrian biblical scholar, tells us in his biography: "We knew nothing about what age we were nor did we understand about germs or illnesses. So we kept healthy and happy."

These Assyrians had no doctors to tell them what was wrong with them. When individuals became sick they simply would tell everyone that they felt tired. There were no long and terrifying mysterious Greek and Roman names for diseases and no fear of incurable illnesses. They had no tangible understanding of the aging process nor were they afraid of lack for their senior years. Their faith was simple. The same God who cared for them today would meet their needs tomorrow.

Turning to Love and Harmony

When we turn to God, our minds become filled with harmonious spiritual forces. We then can sense strength and healing moving in our bodies. It is important to keep our minds clear. When our hearts fill with hatred, grudges, or resentments, we open the door for sickness. The opposite is also true. When our hearts fill with love and harmony, which is another way of saying God's presence, we open the door for health and joy.

The real question is the one that Jesus asked the man who had been ill for a long time. "Are you willing to be healed?" Do we really want to be well? Wholeness comes from a willingness to be whole in spirit, mind, and body.

34

Rivers of Truth

"Now on the greatest day of the festival, which is the last day of the great feast, Jesus was standing, crying out, saying: If anyone thirsts, let him come to me and drink. Everyone who believes in me even as the scriptures have said: Rivers of living water will flow out from within him [literally, from his belly]."[1]

Water Symbolizes Truth

Water is very scarce and precious in the Holy Land. Therefore, Eastern writers represent truth symbolically as "water." Without water no one can live. So truth which is simply "divine realization" is just as necessary for abundant living as water is to life. In the Bible, clear and plentiful water symbolizes spiritual enlightenment. When an individual needs spiritual enlightenment, Near Easterners refer to that person as a "thirsty soul."

When Jesus cried out: "If anyone thirsts, let him come to me and drink," he meant that if anyone lacked spiritual understanding he or she could come to Jesus and learn. "Rivers of living water will flow out of his inner most being" means enlightenment and abundant satisfaction would result from Jesus' teaching. "Believe in me" refers to believing in Jesus' gospel; that is, to have confidence and faith in his joyful message.

---

[1]Jn. 7:37-38, Aramaic Peshitta text.

"Living water" signifies clear running water which is living truth. This living truth, which is practical, manifests in an individual's life as abundance and health.

"There is a river, the streams whereof shall make glad the city of God, the holy place of the tabernacle of the most High."[2] "River" in this verse of the psalm indicates truth, teaching, or simply God's light. The Hebrews called Jerusalem "the city of God" because it means the place of peace and harmony. Metaphysically one can reinterpret the scripture to read: "In the place of peace and harmony (the city of God), there are rivers of truth whose streams make the inner heart glad and exceedingly joyful."

Water from God's Throne

"And he showed me a river of flowing waters pure and clear as rock crystal coming out of God's throne and of the Lamb."[3] (See also Ezekiel 47:1-12.) Clear and pure water represents peace and harmony. Muddy and turbulent water connotes strife and great difficulties.

When God's throne (God's sovereignty) and meekness (the lamb) are fully established in one's consciousness, truth flows clearly and abundantly from one's heart and soul. The scripture plainly says that the "river of flowing waters" comes directly from the throne of God and of the Lamb. There is only one throne, one seat of authority that God and the Lamb share together. This means that there is only one source, one authority

---

[2]Ps. 46:4, KJV.

[3]Rev. 22:1, Aramaic Peshitta text.

from which truth flows. The Lamb represents meekness (a nonviolent life); God represents love. In the book of the Revelation, both God and the Lamb are always the basis for abundance and health. Together, they are the source of life.

35

Sitting in Heaven

"And he [God] has raised us with him and has seated us with him in heaven through Jesus the Messiah that in the oncoming ages, he might make known the exceeding riches of his goodness and his kindness that are upon us through Jesus the Messiah."[1]

Through the powerful resurrection of Jesus, humanity has been raised to a higher level of consciousness—"heaven." Jesus, who was the human sacrifice of religious violence, has revealed to the human family a new way of life. The human race fears and considers death the end of all things. But the truth is that life never knows annihilation. Life knows only transmutation or transformation. When Jesus conquered the grave and unmasked the face of death, he became the way-shower of a new understanding of everlasting life. Humanity no longer needs to fear death.

Idiomatic Meanings

Paul uses the expression "raised us with him." The pronoun "him" refers to Jesus and his resurrection. And it means that God has raised us along with Jesus to a higher level of realization. "Heaven" in this verse signifies a place of peace, harmony, tranquility, and joy. "Sitting in heaven" means we are resting in

---

[1]Eph. 2:6-7, Aramaic Peshitta text.

a state of being that is above the common awareness of life—a state of serenity, understanding, and balance.

A Raised Humanity

The more we become acutely aware of ourselves as "children of God," the more we will sit with God in heaven—that is, enjoying peace of mind and joy of living. There will be no more fear, strife, or wars within ourselves or with others. According to Paul, God initiated this way of life through Jesus, who brought life and immortality to the light for all humanity. And the more we come to know the living, indwelling Christ, the more we discover our own divine nature, which is the genuine essential self. Abundant goodness flows from us through a Christ consciousness. We become exceedingly rich in compassion and kindness through this form of enlightenment.

When the apostle Paul opened his letter to the Ephesians, he said: "Blessed is God the Father of our Lord Jesus the Messiah who has blessed us with all spiritual blessings in heaven through the Anointed."[2] Abundant love, peace, joy, and understanding result in health, prosperity, and happiness. These things are not virtues or attributes but are spiritual blessings that occur in a state of surrender to God (heaven) through an enlightened soul and heart. An enlightened heart is always a grateful and loving heart.

---

[2]Eph. 1:3, Aramaic Peshitta text.

36

Faith Is Substance

In religious circles one often hears the word "faith" bandied around. People frequently say: "If we are to accomplish anything we must do it through faith." The question arises, what is faith?

In the New Testament letter to the Hebrews, we find a definition for the word "faith." The author tells us "Now faith is the substance of things hoped for, the evidence of things not seen."[1] This translation is from the King James Version. However, the Aramaic text renders this verse somewhat differently. "Now faith is the assurance concerning things that we hope for [expect], as it was the substance of things that are now in existence. And it is the appearance [revelation] of things not seen."[2] As one can readily see, the Aramaic text expands the idea of faith.

The Aramaic Root Meaning

Haymanootha is the Aramaic word for "faith." It also means "confidence," "firmness," "truthfulness," "faithfulness," and "trustworthy." This Aramaic word comes from the Semitic root *amen*. *Amen* means "to make firm," "true," "lasting," "never ceasing or ending," "eternal," "perpetual," and "ever."

---

[1]Heb. 11:1, KJV.

[2]Aramaic Peshitta text.

Faith, then, is a firm attitude of mind and heart. It is "firm" in the sense of "true, lasting, and enduring." We must not confuse this idea of being "firm" with stubbornness. It is a quality or attitude of perseverance.

What Is Substance?

"Faith is the substance of things now in existence." Substance means "that of which things consist—matter, material," and literally, "that which stands under." The author of Hebrews teaches that faith itself is what all things are really made of. Faith stands behind or rather "stands under" all things that are in existence.

We often think of things such as cars, money, homes, and other mundane affairs as substance. But the writer tells us that behind all material appearances is "faith." This is the real, genuine substance that "stands under" everything we see. Our faith is the true substance that we possess, and not the "things" we may own. Faith manifests all things.

Projections of Faith

Material goods are projections of faith. This is so because faith is the only true, firm, solid, tangible substance there is! All material things as we now see them will sooner or later disappear. But faith will never disappear. It seems that we are constantly looking for ways to obtain more things, when all the time faith, which is an integral part of us all, is the very substance of the things we desire. Faith is also wholeness and health. Jesus continually reminded those whom he healed that

218

their *"faith had made them whole."*

Faith Evinces Truth

"And what more should I say? For time would fail me to tell about Gideon, Barak, Samson, Jephthah, David, also Samuel and the rest of the prophets, who through faith conquered kingdoms, brought about true justice, obtained promises. . . . became valiant in battle, routed the camps of enemies, while others died through tortures, not hoping for deliverance, that they might have a better resurrection. Others endured mocking and beatings. Still others were handed over to bonds and imprisonment, some were stoned, some were cut apart, some died by the edge of the sword. . . Thus, these all having obtained a testimonial through the faith, did not receive the promise."[3]

Through these passages of scripture we learn that some men and women demonstrated their faith by suffering loss. Others, of course, demonstrated their faith conquering kingdoms. But, both kinds of people confirmed their faith. For we see that faith is the only substance we need. Faith itself is the genuine demonstration of truth and not just our beliefs.

---

[3]Heb. 11:32-39, Aramaic Peshitta text.

37

A Mysterious Personage

"For this Melchizedek, king of Salem, priest of the most high God, who met Abraham returning from the slaughter of the kings, and blessed him; to whom also Abraham gave a tenth part of all; first being by interpretation king of righteousness, and after that also king of Salem, which is, king of peace; without a father, without a mother, without descent, neither having beginning of days, nor end of life; but made like unto the Son of God; abideth a priest continually."[1]

Many Interpretations

This particular scripture from the book of Hebrews has created hundreds of interpretations from the sublime to the bizarre and outlandish. There is much speculation and there are many theories about this man who made his appearance to the Hebrew patriarch Abraham. Some interpreters claim that Melchizedek came from another planet and was a spaceman. Others claim he was some sort of god. Still others believe that this mysterious personage was an appearance of the Christ during the life of Abraham. Many biblical authorities believe Melchizedek was an appearance of Yahweh in human form (a theophany—an appearance of God).

The book of Genesis tells us something about Melchizedek.

---

[1]Heb. 7:1-3, KJV.

In Genesis, chapter 14:18-20, the King James Version reads: "And Melchizedek, king of Salem, brought forth bread and wine; and he was the priest of the most high God. And he blessed him, and said, Blessed be Abraham of the most high God, possessor of heaven and earth; and blessed be the most high God, which hath delivered thine enemies into thy hand. And he [Abraham] gave him tithes of all."

What makes the character of Melchizedek so mysterious is that the author describes him as "without a father, without a mother, without descent, neither having beginning of days, nor end of life." Anyone reading this passage would most naturally conclude that Melchizedek was neither born nor did he ever die. One would also assume that he was a supernatural being because he was "without a father and without a mother." However, this matter changes entirely when reading the Aramaic Peshitta text of the letter to the Hebrews. It reads as follows: "Neither his father, nor his mother are recorded in the family records; and neither the beginning of his days nor the end of his life; but like the Son of God lasts forever."

Melchizedek a Priest of God

According to the Bible, Melchizedek was a priest. It is assumed that he was Chaldean and that he had migrated to Palestine before Abraham had come into the same region. Melchizedek is a Semitic name that combines the words *malka*, "king," and *zedec*, "justice," or "righteousness." Evidently, Melchizedek had settled in southern Palestine in a town called Salem (peace). He worshiped the most high God. In those ancient days, the Bedouin tribal people preferred having a priest-king as a ruler. These small tribes, by having a priest-king, could avoid political strife and excessive taxation. Melchizedek was a priest-king who ruled over the political as well as the spiritual affairs of his tribe. This Chaldean had no written records or recorded genealogy like Aaron, the brother of Moses. And yet Melchizedek was a priest who worshiped the most high God. It was the same God that Abraham worshiped.

Christ and Melchizedek

Thus, the ministry of Jesus as a high priest was compared to the priestly ministry of Melchizedek. The author makes this comparison because Jesus was not descended from any priestly lineage like Aaron's sons. (Moses had ordained Aaron his brother as high priest. All of Aaron's descendants were priests through the family blood line.) How could Jesus be a priest, as he was not a descendant from any priestly line? The ministry of Jesus, according to the writer, was purely spiritual and was a priesthood similar to Melchizedek.

This type of priesthood to which Melchizedek belonged was of the ancient order of priest-kings. Both the author of the Genesis account of Melchizedek and the author of Hebrews did not make any endeavor to trace Melchizedek's lost genealogy. The intent of the writer to the Hebrews was only to compare the ministry of Jesus with the ministry of Melchizedek. One can easily see that a poor translation of Scripture can lead to many unnecessary ideas and concepts.

38

Perfect Love

"There is no fear in love, but perfect love casts out fear, because fear has punishment. And the one fearing has not been perfected in love."[1] The King James Version of this verse of scripture reads almost identically to the Greek interlinear version. However, the Aramaic text reads as follows: "There is no fear in love, but complete love throws out fear. And this is so because fear is terrifying. He, then, who fears has not matured in love."[2] There are two terms that need clarification in this verse and they are the words "perfect" and "love."

The Term "Perfect"

We all have our own ideas of what it means when we use the word "perfect." This is especially true when we talk about "perfect love" or a "perfect relationship." For most people, this word "perfect" can be a troublesome term. It seems that many of us suffer under the tyranny of trying to become perfect. We labor under the idea of trying to live a perfect life.

Perhaps you have made the statement, or heard someone else make the statement, about wanting to be a "perfect parent, brother, sister, or a friend." Many parents attempt to "raise a perfect family." This list can go on and on endlessly. Although

---

[1] 1 Jn 4:18, Greek Interlinear text, Jay P. Green, Sr. translation.

[2] Aramaic Peshitta text.

we make a tremendous effort and aspire with all that is in us to reach some sort of perfection, we almost always fail. Then, we usually agonize under the feelings of guilt, shame, and blame. In my lectures around the country, I sometimes mention to my audience that we all seem to be addicted to a terrible psychic drug called "PCP—Power, Control, and Perfection." So, what does the writer of this epistle mean when he refers to "perfect" love?

An Aramaic Word

John, in his letter, uses the Aramaic term *mshamlya,* coming from the root word *mla*. Its verbal origin means "to fill, replenish, complete, conclude," and also "to come to full growth." Thus, John describes love as "complete," "mature," or "whole." He qualifies this love as a love that is mature, rounded out—a love that is all-inclusive. So we may translate this first part of the verse as: "There is no fear in love, but *complete* (or *mature*) love throws out fear."

The nature of fear terrifies. It torments and alarms us. But the nature of an all-inclusive love cannot hold fear. This kind of love naturally and spontaneously throws it out. So love that includes everything is not afraid of anything.

Of course, this does not mean that we have become "perfect." We cannot cast out fear by becoming perfect. We simply need to mature in love until it thoroughly saturates us. Fear, then, will have no fertile ground in which to grow. Let us now move onto the next word "love."

224

Greek Divisions of Love

First of all, the term "love" even in English is difficult to nail down with a fixed meaning. When we say that "love is such and such," we have limited it. Love is not anything we can really define. It defies and goes beyond any definition we may wish to apply to it. Ancient Greeks divided the word "love" into several categories with distinct Greek terms. There is *Philia* ("family love"), *Eros* ("sexual love"), and *Agape* ("divine love"[3]).

The Aramaic Meaning of Love

The Aramaic language does not divide or compartmentalize the word love, as the Greek language does. Love, in its nature, is always loving. *Hooba,* "love," comes from the Aramaic root *hab* or *hav*. It means "to set on fire" and "to burn fiercely," that is, "to burn so strongly that it turns white hot." Scripture tells us that "God is love." (See 1 John 4:8.) Throughout holy Scripture, various biblical authors symbolize the presence of God as "fire."

Some writers refer to God as a "consuming fire." When the angel of Lord (Yahweh) appeared to Moses on Mt. Sinai, he did so in a fiery bush that did not become consumed. Fire is also a symbol for transformation. It transforms one kind of material substance into another. When we think of the destructive force of fire, it still is transforming one substance into another, even if the fire may change a particular material object or thing into ash.

---

[3]Some modern NT scholars dispute this strict meaning of the Greek word *agape.* They believe it also means sexual and family love. See William E. Phipps, *The Sexuality of Jesus.*

God's presence is nothing but pure love (*hooba*). The Spirit of God is the most compassionate, "white hot," fiery presence we can experience. This love does not discriminate for it loves everyone the same. (See Matthew 5:44-47.) John continues: "My beloved, let us love one another. For Love is from God. Everyone who loves is born of God and knows God. He who does not love does not know God."[4]

Now we can better understand John when he says: "Complete love throws out fear, because fear terrifies." Love is so intense, powerful, and "white hot" that we cannot really describe it at all. Most of the deep things in life often lack definition. This is because they go beyond words and mental comprehension, but never beyond our apprehension. We can apprehend love because love apprehends us! It is the source of our nature—a living energy. Try though we may, we cannot run from it.

We may fear other people's lifestyles and a host of other things in life. But a complete, mature love does not fear anything because it is an all-inclusive love. And an all-inclusive love is God. "Anyone, then, who fears has not matured in love."

---

[4]1 Jn. 4:7-8a, Aramaic Peshitta text.

39

The Book of Revelation

One of the most difficult and doctrinally controversial writings of the Bible is the book of Revelation. Its numerous and puzzling visions and symbols are extremely complicated and troublesome for us to decipher. Literally hundreds of varying and contradictory interpretations of this book exist.

Basically we may interpret it exoterically (from a historical point of view) or esoterically (from a spiritual or metaphysical perspective). One form of interpretation does not invalidate the other. In other words, we can clarify this book from both viewpoints. However, no one individual can claim that his or her particular explanation is the only correct interpretation.

This chapter, of course, is not intended to be an exhaustive study on the Revelation of St. John. It is an Aramaic, Near Eastern approach to the book. It is also a metaphysical look at this revelation. In spite of the many obstacles we must overcome, there are some specific keys that will help us unlock the Revelation. This book has another name—"Apocalypse." The term "Apocalypse" comes from the Greek language. It means "the unveiling."

Keys

We must recognize certain facts before we can begin to open this book. Three key realizations are necessary for us to grasp as we begin.

The First Key: Revelation is a Near Eastern book. It is typically Semitic in its style and character.

The Second Key: It contains more than one thousand symbols, two-thirds of which come directly from the Hebrew Bible (Old Testament) and other Jewish apocryphal and apocalyptic writings. The remaining one-third comes from everyday life experiences of Near Eastern peoples. We must not take these symbols and visions literally. They point to a much larger reality.

To anyone who is familiar with Hebrew Scripture, Jewish apocryphal and apocalyptic books, and ancient Semitic ways of life, the Revelation does not appear strange or mystifying. Mysticism is an aspect of life that Near Easterners readily accept. They do not contend with it on an intellectual level as we usually do in the West.

The Third Key: The author clearly says what the aim of the Revelation is in the first verse of chapter one: "The revelation of Jesus the Anointed which God gave to him to reveal to his servants." Both historically and metaphysically this revelation is an ever-present and individual realization of the Christ awareness. Jesus of Nazareth was the first to make known the revelation of Christhood. Now, according to the book of Revelation, Jesus, as the Anointed (Christ), further unveils to his servants the meaning of Christhood in its broadest scope.

The final apocalypse is not doom and destruction, but the ultimate victory of this very Christ-hood *for* every individual, *in* every individual, and *as* every individual. John in his gospel tells us: "But to those who accept him [the Christ] to them he gave the right [power and authority] to become God's children, to those who believe in his name."[1]

---

[1] Jn 1:12, Aramaic Peshitta text.

A spiritual interpretation of the Revelation describes different modes of consciousness that lead to the total establishment of the Christ individually and universally. Keep in mind that the writer is a mystic. Therefore, his book is mystical. Let us now consider some of the visions and their meanings in the light of Near Eastern biblical symbolism along with their practical spiritual implications.

The Revelation

Giliana is the Aramaic word for "revelation." It implies "vision" and "dream." Its root is *gla* and means "to uncover," "to unveil," "to reveal," "to lay open," "to declare," "to show," and "to make known." Let us remember that the theme of the Revelation is the ultimate triumph of the Christ. How this supreme victory of the Christ comes about is revealed through seven basic visions, each one of which is then divided into seven subordinate visions. The entire structure of the book is in multiples of seven. This is typically Semitic.

Biblical scholars divided all the books of the New Testament into chapters and verses around the 12th and 13th centuries C.E. Revelation contains 22 chapters. Chapter One introduces us to the messenger of the Revelation. Chapters Two and Three contain pastoral admonitions to the seven churches, seven Christian centers in Asia Minor. These two chapters do not address the entire Christian community, only those in Asia minor. Chapters Four through Twenty-two are the seven basic visions and sub-visions, with an epilogue and benedictions.

229

Introduction

Fifteen miles off the coast of Asia Minor near the ancient city of Ephesus, John dictated his revelation to a scribe. He was a prisoner on this island because of witnessing for Jesus, the Messiah. In the opening chapter, the heavenly messenger introduces himself. "And I turned to see the voice that spoke with me. And as I turned, I saw seven golden lampstands."

Numbers in the Bible have more meaning than just their numerical value. Near Eastern people consider the number "seven" as the most sacred number. According to their belief, it signifies perfection and completeness. The seven-branched candlestick (Menorah), for example, once stood in the holy place of the Jewish temple where only priests could enter. In John's vision, the seven golden lampstands represent the seven light centers—the seven churches of Asia Minor.

The lampstand itself with its seven branches also signifies fullness of light. Metaphysically, it means illumination and understanding. The seven branches symbolize love, light, wisdom, truth, power, beauty, and life. Gold denotes purity and originality.

The Raised Christ

Let us continue with John's opening verses. "And in the midst of the golden lampstands, a human being, clothed in a priestly vestment reaching to the feet and fastened around his chest, a golden belt. And his very head and hair were white as wool, white as snow. And his eyes were like a flame of fire. And his feet resembled the fine brass of Lebanon glowing as fired in a furnace, and his voice was like the sound of many waters. And he had in his right-hand seven stars; and from his mouth came a sharp double-edged sword; and his face [especially the forehead and cheeks] was like the sun shining in its power. And when I saw him I fainted. . ."[2]

This splendorous being that John saw in his vision was Jesus of Nazareth in his full, glorified Christhood. Jesus had conquered death and revealed to humanity the magnificent spiritual state of God's creation. This symbolic picture represents a spiritual human being. It signifies a heart and a soul that contain light. It is a state of being that is ever present within each individual. All humanity will come to know the truth of Being through revelation and realization of the Christ.

Symbols of the Raised Christ Interpreted

The detailed descriptions of the clothes and different areas of the body also denote the qualities of a spiritual human being. It is also a description of a person who has risen in consciousness with Christ. "Priestly vestment reaching to the feet and fastened around his chest, a golden belt," depicts the office of a priest-king and signifies spiritual service and dominion. "Head and hair were white as wool, white as snow," represents pure intelligence and wisdom with great strength and understanding. "White" shows age and experience. "Eyes were like a flame of fire" expresses sincerity and conviction, with keen perception and insight. "His feet resembled the fine brass of Lebanon glowing as fired in a furnace," symbolizes strength and endurance. (The brass of Lebanon was famous for its fine quality, durability, and strength.) "His voice was like the sound of many

---

[2]Rev. 1:12-17, Aramaic Peshitta text.

waters," signifies an all-powerful universal message.

"In his right hand were seven stars" connotes complete authority and illumination. "The sharp double-edged sword that came from his mouth" means an eloquent speaker who can solve any problem. "The face was like the sun shining in its power" depicts a transformed heart and soul expressing truth, love, and light in their full strength, glory, and purity.

The Purpose of the Revelation

The original purpose of the Revelation was to inspire and encourage believers in the triumph of truth, justice and love over all violence, injustice, and hatred. John, through his visions, comforted those who were under heavy persecution. He assured them of the ultimate victory of the Christ—the triumphant Lamb of God. These apocalyptic disclosures were not intended to frighten, but to forewarn and to make known coming events. John did not know that in our age, Bible preachers would use this book to threaten people with religious, violent retaliation under God's order. John was dealing with messianic prophecies that had been fulfilled through Jesus of Nazareth. And now the world governments were due for changes and devastating upheavals. God was not threatening the world with judgment. We reap what we sow. He who lives by the sword will perish by the sword. Nations refusing truth will find themselves in the same old violent patterns of the past. The coming of the Christ brought about a change in human thinking. When the fullness of Christ is established within our lives, we experience inward revolutions of heart, mind, soul, and body. This same principle applies to all nations.

The Mark of the Beast

In this Revelation there is a remarkable and frightening vision of vicious beasts and a fiery dragon. One particular vision is the one we call "the mark of the beast." "And he causeth all, both small and great, rich and poor, free and bond, to receive a mark in their right hand, or on their foreheads; and that no man might buy or sell, save he that had the mark, or the name of the beast, or the number of his name. Here is wisdom. Let him that hath understanding count the number of the beast; for it is the number of a man; and his number is six hundred threescore and six [666]."[3]

In Aramaic the expression *khaywat shina* means "wild, female, ferocious beast." There are actually two beasts in the vision; one is a beast from the sea and the other is a land beast. The land beast turns out to be a false prophet (a religious beast). This false prophet gives power to the first beast whose name is 666. The first beast is political power that persecutes truth and justice. Both beasts, historically, represent civil and religious administration of the Roman emperor or any dictatorship that subdues humankind. Esoterically, the beast means any ruthless thought which exalts itself against the Christ awareness. In other words, the beast is a process of reasoning that blinds one's mind to the truth of the Christ nature within. "To receive the mark of the beast on the right hand or forehead" indicates the enslavement of actions (right hand) and mind (forehead) to falsehood, injustice, and violence.

-----

[3]Rev. 13:16-18, KJV.

The Aramaic Code Name

"Here is wisdom. Let him that has understanding count the number of the beast." Writing and sending coded messages was common in biblical days just as it is today. John tells us that only one who has understanding can decipher the code. One has to know the Aramaic, Hebrew, or Greek alphabet to break the secret code name of the beast.

There are many theories and interpretations about the meaning of "the number of the beast." Some suggest that the code is a computer number. They believe that the entire world will come under the control of a universal computer system that will permit or forbid people to buy and sell. This idea could very easily happen, especially in our computer age.

But this is not John's idea in his vision of the beast. John gives us a hint on how to decipher the secret code number. He clearly says that the number is *the name of a man* and not a computer. "For it is the code number *of the name of a man*."

To break the secret code name of the beast one has to know at least one of the three ancient alphabets. We will use the Aramaic alphabet although the Hebrew alphabet is identical to the Aramaic. Every letter of the Aramaic and Hebrew alphabet is a number. Thus, every name or word has a numerical value. Anyone writing in Aramaic or Hebrew will, at the same time, be writing numbers.

For example, the letter "A," *aleph*, is also the number "1." "B," *beth*, is the number "2," and the letter "G," *gamel,* is the number "3." The letters and the numerical figures are written alike. Therefore, the number six-hundred and sixty-six (666) spells a name. Our challenge is to find a name which corresponds exactly to these figures.

The name of the beast in Aramaic is *NRON KSR*, Nero

Caesar. "N" is 50, "R" is 200, "O" is 6, and "N" is 50. "K" is 100, "S" is 60, and "R" is 200. When we add all of these numbers or letters together, the sum is 666 which at the same time spells the name of "Nero Caesar."

The beast is Nero Caesar. He is the one who began the persecution against the Christian movement. This beast represents any political or ecclesiastical authority who acts like Nero and suppresses truth and advocates violence to bring about peace. Esoterically, the number symbolizes human reasoning that seeks to dominate and manipulate others. It is any form of thinking that denies and subjugates ethical and spiritual values for humankind.

We are going to touch on just one more vision of the apocalypse. (It is helpful to bear in mind that the purpose of this revelation was to comfort and encourage all those who were suffering under religious tyranny and persecution.) Let us now move into the last vision and the outcome of the Revelation.

A New Heaven and a New Earth

In my first book, *Let There Be Light: The Seven Keys,* I said that more than 40% of the Bible is based on dreams, visions, and revelations. There is no doubt that the visions and prophecies of Isaiah guided Jesus in his ministry. Of all the prophets, Isaiah gave the clearest picture of the Messiah.

When God appeared to the patriarchs and prophets, he did so through the media of dreams, visions, and revelations. Most of the teachings and instructions that Israel received did not come from holy books but from the hearts and minds of the prophets and spiritual leaders of the time. An inner voice guided these men through their visions and dreams.

The people of Israel had been longing for and expecting a new world order because of the predictions of their prophets. They expected a world leader to protect them and bring peace to all nations. But when Jesus of Nazareth appeared, he did not fulfill their dreams and hopes of a messiah. None of the changes that they were expecting took place with the appearance of the Anointed-Christ.

The truth is that the Romans destroyed Israel as a political force and nation. If Jesus of Nazareth truly was the Messiah, why had not the new world order come into being? Even the Christian movement itself suffered great persecutions. After all, the early Christians were also expecting Jesus to return as the triumphant Messiah.

John, the revelator, was no doubt pondering and wondering about the same unfulfilled prophecies concerning the work of the Messiah. During his meditations and prayers, John received a series of visions which answered the questions of the seemingly unfulfilled messianic prophecies. As I said earlier in this chapter, the book of Revelation was written to encourage those who had embraced the teaching of Jesus. John did not write these visions to put fear and dread into the hearts of sincere seekers of truth.

The Closing Vision

In the closing apocalyptic vision, John saw the fulfillment of the visions and dreams of the prophets. He described his prophetic picture in this manner: "And I saw a new heaven and a new earth. For the very first heaven and the first earth had gone away. Now the sea was no more."[4] John saw a new heaven and earth. However, Isaiah saw the same picture eight hundred years before John recorded his vision in the Revelation.

"For behold I [Yahweh God] create a new heaven and a new earth. And the former things will not be remembered nor come into mind. But my people will be glad and rejoice forever because I am creating."[5] Isaiah, the great Hebrew prophet and statesman, had predicted a new heaven and a new earth, but John, the revelator saw the new heaven and the new earth. This Aramaic phrase means "a new world order." The Messiah's appearance was to bring about that new world order. Jesus' disciples believed that their master was the Messiah, yet the world order did not become new.

A Metaphysical Meaning

On an esoteric level, however, a new world order did begin. But how and when will the new heaven and the new earth appear? What we must understand is that there can be no new order without a new humanity. Humankind must come to a new realization of itself and the universe. Our present world system as we now know it is nothing more than a projection of human consciousness. When the consciousness of humanity changes, then the world order will change naturally and spontaneously.

"A new heaven and new earth," also means a total transformation of heart and mind. "Heaven" symbolically represents the spirit of a human being or the superconscious and higher forms

---

[4]Rev. 21:1, Aramaic Peshitta text.

[5]Isa. 65:17-18, Aramaic Peshitta text.

237

of thinking. "Earth" represents the physical body and the materialistic forms of thinking. "Sea" depicts the soul, the subconscious, and other hidden forms of thinking.

Literally, the heavens and the earth are always renewing themselves. Heaven and earth are always new. So John definitely was referring to a new world order. This could only come about with a change in the hearts and minds of all races.

Enlightened Consciousness

John sees, by revelation, that the coming of the Messiah into the hearts of people transforms their present state of consciousness into a Christ-anointed state (enlightened with God). He indicates that this new mode of being would collapse the former states of heart and mind. This transformation would cleanse the subconscious to such an extent that it would no longer exist: "For there was no more sea." What it means is that there would be no need for hidden subconscious images of the mind.

Outward chaos is a manifestation of a chaotic mind. Order comes from a clear mind immersed in God's presence which is divine order. Paul in his letter to the Corinthians puts this idea forward in a very succinct manner. "Now all who are in Christ are new creations. Old things have passed away. Now all things have become new through God. . ."[6]

The Final Outcome

In the ultimate victory of the Christ, the beast (tyrannical

---

[6]2 Cor. 5:17-18, Aramaic Peshitta text.

political powers), the false prophet (false religious powers), and the devil (deception itself) are thrown into the lake of fire. All those who practice violent deeds, the sinful, the abominable, murderers, idolators, and all liars have their portion in the lake that burns with fire and brimstone. All of this means that the sources of evil and violence with their outlets will cease! A new order begins! It is the ending of a story that really counts. In the case of the Revelation or the Apocalypse, the final outcome is glorious and victorious for justice, truth, liberty, and love.

"And he showed me a pure river of the water of life, clear as rock crystal, gushing out of God's throne and of the Lamb. In the midst of the great street of the city [the new Jerusalem], and on either side of the river, was the tree of life, which bore twelve kinds of fruits, and each month it yielded one of its fruits. And the leaves of the tree were for the healing of the peoples. And that which withers will be no more, but God's throne and the Lamb's will be in it. His servants will serve him. They will see his face, and his name will be on their foreheads. There will be no night there. They will need neither a candle nor the light of the sun. For the Lord God shines on them and they will reign forever and ever."[7]

---

[7]Rev. 22:1-5, Aramaic Peshitta text.

Appendix 1

A Brief History of the English Bible

The "Englishing" of the Hebrew Bible and the New Testament has a long and fascinating history involving both religious and governmental politics. The term "Englishing" was coined when so many different English versions of the Bible were appearing in the British Isles culminating with the Authorized Version of Scripture better known in America as the King James Version of 1611. This writing is a condensed accounting of the origin of our English Bible versions. It was originally written in response to questions I was asked about our English Bible versions during my lectures throughout the United States and Canada.

Christianity and Great Britain

The greatest obstacle to an early English translation of the Bible was the mixing and blending of languages on the isles of Britain. Christianity entered Great Britain sometime in the latter half of the second century. However, it did not take root until three or four centuries later. Ireland became the rich, fertile ground for the growth and expansion of the Christian church. Its progress in the Emerald Isle was so steady that by the sixth century Christianity had spread into Scotland and northern England. During this period of history few could read or write. It was the intense preaching of the gospel by the educated monks and their students who brought the extension of Christianity throughout Britain. At that particular time the language of the church's worship was Latin. Its version of Holy Scripture was also in Latin, the Old Latin Manuscripts.[1]

Pope Damascus in 382 C.E. had commissioned Jerome (342-420) to revise the Old Latin version of the gospels. He used a Greek manuscript as the basis of his revision but did not complete the rest of the New Testament. When Jerome revised what Christians call the "Old Testament," he began with the Psalms. Further work on the other books of the Hebrew Bible were direct translations from Hebrew texts. The work was completed around the latter part of the fourth century. This version, known as the Vulgate, was widely used in the West and its original intent was to end the great textual differences in the Old Latin Manuscript. As the Vulgate superseded the Old Latin version, the latter lost its authority in the church. Let us recall that educated monks interpreted the Latin Bible in the tongues and dialects of their listeners.[2]

---

[1] This Old Latin MSS was a translation of the Hebrew Bible from the Greek Septuagint and not directly from Hebrew texts. The New Testament part of the Old Latin MSS derived from various Greek versions.

[2] For a detailed study of early versions of the Bible see Ernst Wurthwein, *The Text of the Old Testament*; Bruce Manning Metzger, *The Text of the New Testament: its Transmission, Corruption, and Restoration*, also Dr. Metzger — *The Early Versions of the New Testament*; Philip W. Comfort, *Early Manuscripts & Modern Translations of the New Testament*.

Early English Manuscripts

In the middle of the seventh century the earliest beginnings of an English Bible (if one could call it such) made its appearance. Bede (C. 673-735), the great venerable Anglo-Saxon biblical scholar and "Father of English History," was the first known individual to render certain biblical subjects into the Anglo-Saxon tongue beginning with the creation story.

In South England there was a zealous monk whose name was Aldhelm, (D. 709). He became the Abbot of Malmesbury about 675 and in 705 the first Bishop of the new diocese of Sherborne. Aldhelm was also an outstanding musician. According to English historians, he was the first known translator of the Psalms into Anglo-Saxon English. We are told that the people of South England received their "*religious instruction through popular poetry attuned to the harp of Aldhelm. This shrewd official observed that the usual sermon had little attraction for the ordinary run of Englishmen. Being a skillful musician, he put on the garb of a minstrel and took up a position on a bridge over which many people were obliged to pass. His artistic playing soon attracted a group of listeners. As soon as he had thus collected an audience he gave his music and words a religious turn, and by the strains of his splendid instrument and the persuasive form of his attractive language won many to Christianity.*" [3]

Then there appeared Richard Rolle of Hamplole (1300-1349) who translated the Psalms into the Middle English and wrote commentaries on the same. He was known as a hermit and mystic. About that same time the biblical works of William of Shoreham became popular. "*The spread of the Shoreham-Rolle*

---

[3]Price, *The Ancestry of Our English Bible*, p. 226.

versions of the Psalter was the beginning of the triumph of the English language proper." These two translations of the Psalms initiated a strong craving throughout Great Britain for more translations of the Bible.

English Translations Forbidden

Incredible as this seems Pope Innocent III, in 1199, had declared that: "*The secret mysteries of the faith ought not to be explained to all men in all places, since they cannot be everywhere understood by all men.*" Then Pope Gregory VII followed Innocent III with: "*Not without reason has it pleased Almighty God that Holy Scripture should be a secret in certain places, lest, it were plainly apparent to all men, perchance it would be little esteemed and be subject to disrespect; or it might be falsely understood by those of mediocre learning and lead to error.*" But despite these declarations of Ecclesiastical powers, translation of Scripture could not be stopped. Humanity desired to drink from the fountains of knowledge that had been hidden from them by those in authority. The religious dam that held back the flood waters of English translations was about to crack.

The Wycliffe Version

In the fourteenth century, a period of great political and sociological transition and ecclesiastical controversies, John Wycliffe, scholar and lecturer at Oxford, translated the Bible from Latin into English. He translated the New Testament about 1380 and in 1382 Wycliffe finished the entire Bible. Other scholars under the direction of Wycliffe worked on the translation of the Old Testament. In reality, his devoted disciples and co-workers completed most of the Old Testament translation. Wycliffe died two years after the completion of the Bible in 1382. His translation was stilted and mechanical. The language of his work, a Midland dialect, did not represent the central strand of development in English. Almost immediately, Wycliffe's version needed revision and it was undertaken not long after his death.

The Response

What was the reaction of the religious world? What did Church authorities have to say about this translation of Holy Scripture? Archbishop Arundel in 1412, when writing the Pope concerning Wycliffe, said: ". . .*that wretched and pestilent fellow of damnable memory, the very herald and child of anti-Christ, who crowned his wickedness by translating the Scriptures into the mother tongue.*" A provincial council at Oxford early in the 15th century made this remark: "*No one shall in the future translate on his own authority any text of Holy Scriptures into the English tongue — nor shall any man read this kind of book, booklet or treatise, now recently composed in the time of the said John Wycvliffe or later, or any that shall be composed in the future, in whole or part, publicly or secretly under a penalty of the greater Excommunication.*" Did this decree put out the flaming desire to see the light of Scripture translated into the common tongue of English?

The Renaissance

Then, in the fifteenth century, that great epoch of awakening, the West experienced the Renaissance. Its first powerful stirring occurred in Italy under the guidance of certain free thinkers and writers of that country. No one was able to hold back the tide of change and the profound forces at work in Europe's fermenting culture. These aggressive and compelling energies were impacting the church. It could not escape them. Thus, another translator by the name of William Tyndale (1494? - 1536), because of persecution in England, had to cross over to the Continent to translate the Bible into English. Tyndale was a Greek scholar and had access to the Greek text of Erasmus and other biblical writing which Wycliffe did not possess. He was martyred before he completed the Old Testament. In the ensuing days religious powers shed much blood. But, because of the "new birth movement" in that age, Ecclesiastical walls of ignorance and fear could not hold back the rising flood of translations of the Bible into English.

More English Versions

Next came Miles Coverdale (1488-1568), a friend of Tyndale. This version was based on Tyndale's translation of Scripture with some help from the Latin text and other versions. Then the Matthew's Bible made its appearance. This version was based on the work of Tyndale and Coverdale; that is, it was a revision of the work of Tyndale, pieced out with Tyndale's unpublished manuscripts and portions of Coverdale's Old Testament. The editor of this version was John Rogers (1500-1555). He was the first British Protestant Martyr under Queen

Mary. In 1537 under the name of Thomas Matthew, he published the first complete version of the Bible in English.

In 1539, the Great Bible made its showing. This also was based on other English versions which had preceded it, that is, Matthew's, Coverdale's and Tyndale's translations. This Bible version won out among all other English versions and was *"appointed to the use of the Churches."* For nearly 30 years (except in the reign of Queen Mary) it was the only version that could lawfully be used in England. It is very important to remember the name of this Bible because the King James Version derived its so called "translation" not only from the Great Bible but, as you will see, from the Bishops Bible as well.

The Counter Reformation

Under Queen Mary a counter reformation began to take hold in England and many Protestant scholars took refuge in Geneva. Thus, in 1560, the Geneva version of the Bible came into existence. This translation was a revision of the Great Bible and other English reworked versions of Scripture. Interestingly, it was this Geneva English version of the Bible that the Puritans brought with them to the shores of America. Its biblical annotations were strongly Protestant and leaned heavily toward Calvinism.[4]

---

[4]John Calvin, 1509-1564, French reformer and theologian who was also thought of, by certain individuals, as a "theocratic tyrant." Calvinism is a theological system formulated by John Calvin. He strongly advocated the absolute authority of the Bible, that the State must be subject to the Church and many other biblical doctrinal beliefs.

Shakespeare quoted the Geneva Bible in his works. It was after meditation on the Geneva translation that John Bunyan wrote his famous *Pilgrims Progress*. The Geneva version became very popular. Then, the Archbishop of Canterbury, along with other bishops during the reign of Queen Elizabeth, decided to make a revision of the Great Bible of 1539. Because of the popularity of the Geneva Bible, these bishops made their decision for a revision. This "new" translation—or, more properly, revision—became known as the Bishops' Bible of 1568.

The Authorized Version

James Stuart of Scotland, since 1603 King of England, ordered that a new "Revision" be made of the Bishops Bible. Let us recall that the Bishops Bible is a revision of the Great Bible which was based on other English translations and revisions of the Bible. This work was immediately begun by 47 scholars under the authorization of King James.

In 1611 the new version made its appearance. Although the title page described it as *"newly translated out of the original tongues,"* this statement was not entirely in accord with the facts. The translation was actually a revision of the Bishops Bible on the basis of the Hebrew and Greek texts. And what is most interesting is that the King James Version of the Bible did not win immediate universal acceptance. It took almost 50 years to displace the popularity of the Geneva Bible.

Let us review: The King James Version was a revision of the Bible based on the Bishops version which was a revision of the Great Bible. The Great Bible was a revision based on Matthew's, Coverdale's and Tyndale's translations and revisions. The history of the English versions of the Bible has not ended because in the 19th and 20th centuries the English-speaking world has become inundated with English versions of Scripture. What are the names of some of these new Bible translations and versions?

The Deluge of English Versions

We have the Revised Standard version, the American Standard version, the New English Bible, the TANAKH (the new Jewish Publication Society translation according to the traditional text), the New American Bible, the Jerusalem Bible, the NIV translation, the Amplified, the Weymouth version, the Moffatt Bible, the Wuest Expanded version and many others too numerous to record. Most of the 20th century English versions of Scripture are translated works from Hebrew and Greek texts. Old Testament translations into English are usually works from the 10th century Hebrew Massoretic text.[5] New Testament English translations usually derive from various Greek texts and versions.

In 1957 there appeared for the first time a complete translation of the entire Old and New Testaments into English from the Aramaic, Semitic Peshitta texts (5th and 6th centuries). This translation is also known as the *Holy Bible from Ancient*

---

[5]This text was name after the Massoretes — Jewish grammarians who worked on the Hebrew text between the 6th and 10th centuries. There is a Greek rendering of the Hebrew text known as the Septuagint. It is the most influential of the Greek versions of the Heb. OT. Jewish tradition attributes its origin to the initiative of Ptolemy Philadelphus (285-246 BCE).

Eastern Manuscripts by George M. Lamsa, Th.D., F.R.S.A. Dr. Lamsa claimed there are about ten to twelve thousand differences or variants between these Aramaic manuscripts and those of the Hebrew and Greek texts of the Bible. Aramaic was the language of Jesus and was the common tongue of Palestine in the first century.

Our Modern World

In the last forty years, and especially in the last three decades, significant changes have taken place in the field of biblical scholarship. New methodologies for exegesis and translating Scripture have now come into play. These modern and current sociological and historical methods provide us with the necessary tools to carefully analyze the social and historical context of biblical narratives. The present research and scholarship draw on biblical and extra-biblical evidence to help us understand the people of biblical lands, their customs and their faith. There is an ongoing explosion of pertinent information in the fields of religion, philology, sociology, archaeology and ancient history that has uncovered the early world of Mesopotamia and the basic social and religious structure of first century Palestine.

Our present knowledge of Aramaic and Hebrew usage of words, idioms and special religious and philosophical terminology has clarified many obscure passages of Scripture. Discovery and work on the Dead Sea Scrolls has aided biblical scholars in their perception and presentation of the overall Jewish background of the times and will continue to yield more information.[6]

Today, in the Western world, there is a greater comprehensive knowledge of Eastern people culturally and psychologically than in the past. Many native born Near Eastern authors have helped us realize the unique thought patterns of Semitic peoples, and their customs and mannerisms that are so distinct from our ways of life. As our understanding of the Near Eastern world increases, especially of biblical days, so will our English translations of the Bible reflect our new comprehension.

---

[6]The Dead Sea Scrolls were hidden in desert caves by Jews as they fled Roman soldiers in 68 C.E.

Appendix 2

The Aramaic Language
A Brief History

The Aramaic language made its historical appearance toward the end of the second millennium B.C.E., in Mesopotamia —the fertile crescent of the ancient Near East. Gradually, at the onset of the first millennium B.C.E., the written and spoken form of the Aramaic tongue began making inroads throughout Near Eastern lands. It was the language of the Arameans, Assyrians, Chaldeans, Hebrews, and Syrians.

Historians tell us that the term "Aramaic," *Aramaya* derives from "Aram." According to Hebrew Scripture, Aram was the grandson of Noah.[1] Aramaic is a Semitic (more precisely, Shemitic) language.[2] The word Aram forms from an Aramaic noun and adjective: *Araa* meaning "earth," "land," "terrain," and *Ramtha* meaning "high."

The fertile valley, Pandan-Aram (Mesopotamia)[3] was the territory in which the descendants of Aram dwelt and in which Aramaic developed and remained pure. In the course of time, because of the practicality of its alphabet and simplicity of style

---

[1]Gen. 10:22-23

[2]Shemitic derives from the name "Shem," the son of Noah. See Gen. 5:32. The expression "Semitic" applies not only to various Semitic dialects but to all the descendants of Shem: the Akkadians, Arameans, Assyrians, Chaldeans, Hebrews and Arabs.

[3]*Beth Nahareen* (Aramaic), *Bet Naharaim* (Hebrew) — "the land between the rivers."

253

in writing and speaking, it attracted all classes of people, government officials, merchants and writers. Thus, by the eighth-century B.C.E., Aramaic became the common tongue among the majority of Semitic clans and was the major language from Egypt to Asia Minor to Pakistan.

Great Semitic empires such as Assyria and Chaldea (Babylon) spoke and wrote in this tongue. It was also the language of the Persian (Iranian) government in its Western provinces. In today's world, among the Chaldeans, Assyrians, Jews, and other Semitic communities in the Near and Middle East, Australia, the United States, and elsewhere, Aramaic continues to be their written and spoken language. Most of these communities regularly speak Aramaic at home, in their social, political, domestic meetings, and in their religious worship — liturgies.

Israel and Aramaic

Biblical as well as secular history records the various expulsions of the twelve tribes of Israel from their homeland to Assyria and Chaldea. Historically, the two most important exiles were in 721 B.C.E. and in 587 B.C.E. In the first exile, 721 B.C.E., the Assyrians took the ten Northern tribes of the House of Israel captive to Nineveh and scattered them throughout Mesopotamia (Northern Iraq, Afghanistan, and Pakistan). These warring conquerors repopulated Northern Israel with some of their own people and other Semitic clans who spoke Aramaic in its Assyrian dialect. (Eastern Aramaic was divided into two dialects, the Northern vernacular spoken in Assyria and the Southern vernacular spoken in Chaldea—Babylon.)

These new inhabitants of the Northern sector of Palestine

254

intermarried with the remnant of Israelites that were left behind by the invading armies of Assyria. The descendants of these mixed marriages came to be known as Samaritans. In the second exile, 587 B.C.E., Nebuchanessar, the Chaldean king, deported the remaining two tribes of the House of Judah, the Southern Kingdom of Israel, to Babylon.

Then in 539 B.C.E., Cyrus, the ruler of Persia (Iran) conquered the great city of Babylon and ended the Chaldean empire's rule. The Persian king granted freedom to the exiled Jews who were living in Babylon. They could now return to Palestine under the protection of the Persian power. By this time, the Jewish people who returned to their homeland were speaking the Southern dialect of Aramaic. Therefore, during the first century in Palestine, the people of Judea spoke in the Southern dialect of Aramaic. But in Galilee Jesus, his disciples, followers, and contemporaries spoke in the Eastern, Northern dialect of Aramaic.[4] Interestingly, the manner of speech, the phraseology, the idioms, and the orientation in the four gospels (Matthew, Mark, Luke, and John) are vividly and distinctively Aramaic. The constant repetitions are characteristic of Semitic Near Eastern speech patterns. Such phrases as *Amen, amen, amar'a lhon*—"Truly, truly, I say to you"—or "In those days," "And it came to pass," "And he said to them," are peculiarly Aramaic.

In some areas of the Holy Land during this period, people spoke Hebrew. Nonetheless, there is some discussion among present day scholars as to its widespread use during the first century C.E. Usually in the synagogues, a reader would read from the scrolls in Hebrew and then interpret it in Aramaic. These interpretations are known as *targumim*. Leaders of the

---

[4]Mk. 14:70.

synagogue had to interpret and teach in Aramaic. As far as we know there were no Greek *targumim*—"interpretations."

Greek and Aramaic

Alexander the Great had conquered the Near East in 330 B.C.E. After Alexander's death in Chaldea, four of his generals divided the Near Eastern lands among themselves. Palestine became a part of that division. The Greeks were Gentile pagans who despised the religion of the Jews. They persecuted and killed the Jews unmercifully. But in 66 B.C.E., Pompey, the famous Roman general and statesman, conquered Eastern Asia Minor, Syria, and Palestine. He, of course, put these conquered lands immediately under Roman rule.

In the time of Jesus, there were ten cities known as the Decapolis. These cities were located east and northeast of the Jordan River as far as Damascus and were independent of Galilee and Judea. The majority of their inhabitants were Gentiles and it is believed that Greek was the predominant language. Therefore, the Greek tongue was also known in Palestine.[5] Be that as it may, the first century evidence clearly indicates that Aramaic was the most common language that the people used throughout Palestine.[6] The message of Jesus of Nazareth was proclaimed and taught all over Palestine, Lebanon, Syria, and Mesopotamia in the Aramaic tongue.

---

[5]See J. N. Sevenster, *Do You Know Greek?* "How Much Greek Could the First Jewish Christians Have Known?," Leiden: E. J. Brill 1968.

[6]See J. Fitzmyer, *A Wandering Aramean: Collected Aramaic Essays*, "The Language of Palestine," pp. 29-56.

Aramaic and Arabic

Aramaic remained the common language of the Near East until the seventh century C.E.; then Arabic gradually began to supplant Aramaic. Nonetheless, the Christians of Iraq, Iran, Syria, Turkey, and Lebanon kept the Aramaic language alive domestically, scholastically, and liturgically. In spite of the pressure of the ruling Arabs to make them speak Arabic, Aramaic still finds utterance in its many dialects, especially among the Assyrians and Chaldeans. Scholars refer to Aramaic as Syriac but this is a misnomer. Syriac is the Greek term for Aramaic[7] Among the Chaldeans and Assyrians today, when they talk about their Semitic language they do not call it Syriac but *Aramaya*—Aramaic. Western scholars have taught these people to refer to their language as *Suriaya*—Syriac.

Concluding Remark: A Tribute

There is just one final aspect of the Aramaic language I wish to mention—its use as the major tongue for the birth and spread of spiritual and intellectual ideas all over the Near East and finally all over the world. Professor Franz Rosenthal, an outstanding Aramaic and Arabic scholar, made the following tribute to the Aramaic language:

> In my view, the history of Aramaic represents the purest triumph of the human spirit as embodied in language

---

[7]See Philip K. Hitti, *The Near East in History*, "The Aramaic Language." For a detailed account of the language, see Rocco A. Errico, *The Message of Matthew: An Annotated Parallel Aramaic-English Gospel of Matthew*, Appendix 1, pp.123-128.

257

(which is the mind's most direct form of physical expression) over the crude display of material power. . .Great empires were conquered by the Aramaic language, and when they disappeared and were submerged in the flow of history, that language persisted and continued to live a life of its own. . The language continued to be powerfully active in the promulgation of spiritual matters. It was the main instrument for the formulation of religious ideas in the Near East, which then spread in all directions all over the world. . . The monotheistic groups continue to live on today with a religious heritage, much of which found first expression in Aramaic.[8]

---

[8]Franz Rosenthal, "Aramaic Studies During the Past Thirty Years," in *The Journal of Near Eastern Studies*, pp. 81-82, Chicago 1978.

Bibliography

I have divided the bibliography into three sections: (1) A general bibliography; (2) A bibliography on the study of Jesus' parables and the historical Jesus; (3) Biblical texts and manuscripts.

(1) General Bibliography

Ackroyd, P. R. & Evans, C. E., *The Cambridge History of the Bible*, London, Cambridge University Press, 1970.

Black, Matthew, *Aramaic Approach to the Gospels and Acts*, Oxford: Clarendon Press, 3rd ed. 1967.

Brettler, Marc Zvi, *The Creation of History in Ancient Israel*, NY, Routledge, 1995.

Burkitt, F., *Early Eastern Christianity: St. Margaret's Lectures 1904, The Syriac Speaking Church*, N.Y., E. P. Dutton & Co., 1904.

Burney, C. F., *The Aramaic Origin of the Fourth Gospel*, London: Oxford University Press, 1922.

Charlesworth, James H., Editor, *The Messiah: Developments in Earliest Judaism and Christianity*, Augsburg Fortress, 1992.

Chilton, Bruce, *Pure Kingdom: Jesus' Vision of God*, Wm.. B. Eerdmans Publishing Co., 1996.

259

Errico, Rocco A., *Setting a Trap for God: The Aramaic Prayer of Jesus*, Unity Village, MO, Unity Books, 1997.

_____, *Let There Be Light: The Seven Keys*, Revised and Expanded Edition, Noohra Foundation, Smyrna, GA (formerly: Santa Fe, NM), 1994.

_____, *Mysteries of Creation: The Genesis Story*, Noohra Foundation, Smyrna, GA (formerly: Santa Fe, NM), 1992.

_____, *The Message of Matthew: An Annotated Parallel Aramaic-English Gospel of Matthew*, Noohra Foundation, Smyrna, GA (formerly: Santa Fe, NM), 1991.

Errico, Rocco A. & Lamsa, George M. *Aramaic Light on the Gospel of Matthew*, Smyrna, GA, Noohra Foundation, 2000.

_____, *Aramaic Light on the Gospels of Mark and Luke*, Smyrna, GA, Noohra Foundation, 2001.

_____, *Aramaic Light on the Gospel of John*, Smyrna, GA, Noohra Foundation, 2002.

Fiorenza, Elisabeth Schussler, *In Memory of Her: A Feminist Theological Reconstruction of Christian Origins*, NY, Crossroad, Tenth Anniversary Edition, 1994.

Fitzmyer, Joseph A., *Essays on the Semitic Background of the New Testament*, London: Society of Biblical Literature and Scholars Press, 1974.

_____, *A Wandering Aramean: A Collection of Aramaic Essays*, Chico, CA, Scholars Press, 1979.

Freedman, David Noel, Editor in Chief, *The Anchor Bible Dictionary*, Doubleday, 1992.

Herklots, H. G. G., *How Our Bible Came to us*, NY, Oxford University Press, 1954.

Hoyt, Edyth Armstrong, *Studies in the Apocalypse of John of Patmos*, Ann Arbor: Edwards Brothers, 1944.

Kenyon, Sir Frederic, *Our Bible and the Ancient Manuscripts*, NY, Harper & Bros. 1958.

Lamsa, George M., *The Shepherd of All: The 23rd Psalm*, Aramaic Bible Center, San Antonio, Texas (Now known as Noohra Foundation, Smyrna, Georgia) 1966.

Lapide, Pinchas, *The Sermon on the Mount: Utopia or Program for action?*, Orbis Books, 1986.

McNicol, Allan J., with Dungan, David L., and Peabody David B., Editors, *Beyond the Q Impasse – Luke's Use of Matthew: A Demonstration by the Research team of the International Institute for Gospel Studies*, Trinity Press, 1996.

Price, Ira Maurice, *The Ancestry of Our English Bible: An Account of Manuscripts, Texts and Versions of the Bible*, NY, Harper & Brothers, 1956.

Rihbany, Abraham M., *The Syrian Christ*, Boston, Houghton Mifflin Co., 1916.
_____, *The Hidden Treasure of Rasmola*, Boston, Houghton Mifflin Co., 1914.
_____, *The Five Interpretations of Jesus*, Boston, Houghton Mifflin Co., 1940.

Tolstoy, Leo, *the Kingdom of God Is Within You: Christianity Not as a Mystic Religion but as a New Theory of Life*, University of Nebraska Press, 1984.

Vermes, Geza, *Jesus and the World of Judaism*, Fortress Press edition, 1984.

Wright, Fred H., *Manners and Customs of Bible Lands*, Chicago, Moody Press, 1953.

(2a) Bibliography: The Parables of Jesus

Donahue, John R., S. J., *The Gospel in Parable*, Fortress Press, 1988.

Ford, Richard Q., *The Parables of Jesus: Recovering the Art of Listening*, Fortress Press, 1997.

Funk, Robert W., *Parables and Presence*, Fortress Press, 1982.
_____, (Jesus Seminar), *The Parables of Jesus*, Polebridge Press, 1994.
_____, *Jesus as Precursor*, Polebridge Press, 1988.

Jeremias, Joachim, *The Parables of Jesus*, Second Revised Edition, Prentice Hall, 1972.

Scott, Bernard Brandon, *Jesus, Symbol-Maker for the Kingdom*, Fortress Press, 1981.
_____, *Hear Then the Parable*, Fortress Press, 1990.

Westermann, Claus, *The Parables of Jesus: In the Light of the Old Testament*, Fortress Press, 1990.

Williams, James G., *Gospel Against Parable: Mark's Language of Mystery*, Almond Press, Sheffield, England, 1985.

Young, Brad H., *Jesus and His Jewish Parables: Rediscovering the Roots of Jesus' Teaching*, Paulist Press, 1989.

(2b) Bibliography: The Historical Jesus

Charlesworth, James H., *Jesus Within Judaism: New Light from Exciting Archaeological Discoveries*, Doubleday, 1988.

Chilton, Bruce and Evan, Craig A., Editors, *Studying the Historical Jesus: Evaluations of the State of Current Research*, Brill, 1998.

Crossan, John Dominic, *The Historical Jesus: The Life of a Mediterranean Jewish Peasant*, San Francisco, Harper, 1991.

Funk, Robert W., (Jesus Seminar) *The Five Gospels*, Polebridge Press, 1993.

Johnson, Luke Timothy, *The Real Jesus: The Misguided Quest for the Historical Jesus and the Truth of the Traditional Gospels*, San Francisco, Harper, 1996.

Meier, John P., *A Marginal Jew: Rethinking the Historical Jesus*, Vol. 1 Doubleday, 1991 and Vol. 2, Doubleday, 1994.

Sanders, E. P., *Jesus and Judaism*, Fortress Press, 1985.

Stanton, Graham, *Gospel Truth? New Light on Jesus and the Gospels*, Trinity Press, 1995.

Wilson, Ian, *Jesus: The Evidence*, Harper & Row, San Francisco, 1988.

Zeitlin, Irving M., *Jesus and the Judaism of His Time*, Polity Press, 1988.

(3) Biblical Texts and Manuscripts

The Hebrew Bible, Masoretic Text, Biblia Hebraic (BHA), Stuttgarensia, 1983.

The New Testament, P'shitta Text, Classical Eastern (Assyrian-Chaldean) Aramaic script, Mosul, Baghdad, 1950.

About the Author

Dr. Rocco A. Errico is an ordained minister, international lecturer and author, spiritual counselor, and one of the nation's leading Biblical scholars working from the original Aramaic *Peshitta* texts. For ten years he studied intensively with Dr. George M. Lamsa, Th.D., (1890-1975), world-renowned Assyrian biblical scholar and translator of the *Holy Bible from the Ancient Eastern Text.* Dr. Errico is proficient in Aramaic and Hebrew exegesis, helping thousands of readers and seminar participants understand how the Semitic context of culture, language, idioms, symbolism, mystical style, psychology, and literary amplification—the *Seven Keys* that unlock the Bible—are essential to understanding this ancient spiritual document.

Dr. Errico is the recipient of numerous awards and academic degrees, including a Doctorate in Philosophy from the School of Christianity in Los Angeles; a Doctorate in Divinity from St. Ephrem's Institute in Sweden; and a Doctorate in Sacred Theology from the School of Christianity in Los Angeles. In 1993, the American Apostolic University College of Seminarians awarded him a Doctorate of Letters. He also holds a special title of Teacher, Prime Exegete, *Maplana d'miltha dalaha*, among the Federation of St. Thomas Christians of the order of Antioch.

Dr. Errico is a featured speaker at conferences, symposia, and seminars throughout the United States, Canada, Mexico and Europe and has been a regular contributor for over 23 years to *Science of Mind Magazine* (circulation: 150,000), a monthly journal founded in 1927. He began his practice as an ordained minister and pastoral counselor in the mid-1950s and during the next three decades served in churches and missions in Missouri, Texas, Mexico, and California. Throughout his public work, Dr. Errico has stressed the nonsectarian, *open* interpretation of Biblical spirituality, prying it free from 2000 years of rigid orthodoxy, which, according to his research, is founded on incorrect translations of the original Aramaic texts.

In 1970, Dr. Errico established the Noohra Foundation in San Antonio, Texas, as a non-profit, non-sectarian spiritual-educational organization devoted to helping people of all faiths to understand the Near Eastern background and Aramaic interpretation of the Bible. In 1976, Dr. Errico relocated the Noohra Foundation in Irvine, California, where it flourished for the next 17 years. For seven years, the Noohra Foundation operated in Santa Fe, New Mexico, and in September 2001, it relocated to Smyrna, Georgia, where Dr. Errico is Dean of Biblical Studies for Dr. Barbara King's School of Ministry—Hillside Chapel and Truth Center.

Under the auspices of the Noohra Foundation, Dr. Errico continues to lecture for colleges, civic groups and churches of various denominations in the United States, Canada, Mexico and Europe.

For a complimentary catalog of Aramaic Bible translations, books, audio and video cassettes, and a brochure of classes, retreats and seminars, or for any other inquiries, write or call the Noohra Foundation. Those interested in scheduling Dr. Errico for a personal appearance may also contact:

Noohra Foundation
PMB 343
4480H South Cobb Drive
Smyrna, GA 30080

Phone: 770-319-9376
Fax: 770-319-9793

Email: info@noohra.com
Noohra Foundation website: www.noohra.com

In addition to *And There Was Light*, the Noohra Foundation is pleased to offer the following books and commentaries by Dr. Rocco A. Errico and Dr. George M. Lamsa.

Commentaries by Dr. Errico and Dr. Lamsa

ARAMAIC LIGHT ON THE GOSPEL OF MATTHEW
(Aramaic New Testament Series Volume 1)

This inimitable commentary acts as a Near Eastern guide, taking you through the heart of the gospels, illuminating difficult and puzzling passages and offering unparalleled insight into the character and behavior of Near Eastern Semites. This volume is more than just a revision of Dr. Lamsa's commentaries, *Gospel Light* and *More Light on the Gospels*. Dr. Errico has edited, expanded and annotated these previous works and added unpublished material that the two of them had drafted just before Dr. Lamsa died in 1975. Dr. Errico completed the comments that they had only outlined and also included information derived from his continual research in Aramaic word meanings and Near Eastern Semitic Studies. $29.95

ARAMAIC LIGHT ON THE GOSPELS OF MARK AND LUKE
(Aramaic New Testament Series Volume 2)

Like the previous volume, this commentary carries you back almost two thousand years, providing a clear perspective of Jesus in the light of his own language, people and times. However, this volume is unique in that it provides insight into the psychology of Jesus' healing methods. $26.95

ARAMAIC LIGHT ON THE GOSPEL OF JOHN
(Aramaic New Testament Series Volume 3)

Dr. Errico and Dr. Lamsa bring clarity and understanding to the most popular (and most misunderstood) gospel. In the 3rd volume of this series, you will learn the Semitic meanings behind such terms as "the

Word," "Light," "Life," "Christ," "Only Begotten." You will also come to understand what Jesus meant when he said "No man comes to the Father except through me" and many other sayings that appear to be sectarian and exclusive. $26.95

ARAMAIC LIGHT ON THE ACTS OF THE APOSTLES
(Aramaic New Testament Series Volume 4)

The book of Acts comes alive under this skillful and cultural approach of Dr. Errico and Dr. Lamsa. They bring clarification to many misunderstood verses of scripture and episodic experiences of the apostles and growth of Jesus' spiritual movement under apostolic guidance. Topics include: *The Ascension of Jesus, Pentecost and the Descent of the Holy Spirit, Paul's Conversion, Healing Methods*, and more. $21.95

ARAMAIC LIGHT ON ROMANS — 2 CORINTHIANS
(Aramaic New Testament Series Volume 5)

This volume presents new insights into and understanding of Paul's letters, his use of Semitic, idiomatic expressions, admonitions and teachings, clarifying many misunderstood statements and teachings that Paul discusses in his epistles, such as: *The True Righteousness of God; Circumcision; Paul's Use of Sacrificial, Cultic Terminology; Paul's Intended meaning of "all have sinned and come short of the glory of God"; The Manifestation of the Sons of God; Speaking in Tongues of Angels and of Men; Women Keeping Silent in Church; Cup of Devils; Long and Short Hair; How Moses Brought Water from a Rock; The Love Chapter.* $24.95

Books by Dr. Errico:

LET THERE BE LIGHT: THE SEVEN KEYS

The Bible is more than anything else a Near Eastern account of spiritual events and teachings. In this illuminating work, Dr. Errico builds a bridge between Western ways of understanding and the Near Eastern social realities that are embedded in the Bible. He helps us to see the Bible through Semitic, Aramaic eyes. Bypassing doctrinal creeds and rigid interpretations, he corrects numerous errors and misleading literal translations that have caused confusion for centuries. This book equips the reader with seven key insights to understand the allusions, parables, and teachings of the Bible, opening the door to the ancient Aramaic world from which the Bible emerged. $17.95

SETTING A TRAP FOR GOD: The Aramaic Prayer of Jesus

A revised and expanded version of Dr. Errico's most popular book—his translation (with commentary) of the Lord's Prayer. Using his own translation directly from the original Aramaic source, Dr. Errico interprets the prayer in terms of eight attunements that align us to spiritual forces in and around us, which is precisely how Jesus taught his disciples to tune in to the inexhaustible power of the Heavenly Father. What exactly does the word "prayer" mean? What does it accomplish? Dr. Errico focuses on original Aramaic manuscripts and the ancient culture of the Near East as he answers these questions. Discover the way of peace, health, and prosperity as you learn to "set a trap" for the inexhaustible power of God. $10.95

THE MYSTERIES OF CREATION: The Genesis Story

A challenging new look at the processes and mysteries of the primal creation account. Dr. Errico uses his own direct translation from the Aramaic-Peshitta text of Genesis 1:1-31 and 2:103. He discusses the Semitic meaning, names and theories of the origin of God. Where appropriate, Dr. Errico borrows insights from the world of both quantum physics and biblical scholarship. He shows readers that behind the material appearance of the world operates a sacred intelligence (called *Elohim*) and that all creation is a meaningful representation of the creative acts of this primal deity. *The Genesis Story* introduces to humankind its responsibility to the earth and its environment. $16.95

THE MESSAGE OF MATTHEW: An Annotated Parallel Aramaic-English Gospel of Matthew

Dr. Errico's stirring translation of the ancient Aramaic Peshitta text of Matthew is further enriched with his stimulating and illuminating annotations. The style of writing in *The Message of Matthew* is simple and direct. The English translation is printed on the left side of the page with footnotes. The Aramaic text is printed on the right with additional footnotes in English. These valuable footnotes explain the meanings of Aramaic words and customs with supplementary historical information. $24.95

CLASSICAL ARAMAIC: Book I (with Father Michael Bazzi)

Learn to read and write the language of Jesus in a self-teachable format. Classical Aramaic is a practical grammar that prepares you to read the New Testament in Jesus' own native tongue. $24.95

LA ANTIGUA ORACIÓN ARAMEA DE JESÚS: El Padrenuestro

Dr. Errico's own translation into Spanish of his book *The Ancient Aramaic Prayer of Jesus.* $8.95

ACHT EINSTIMMUNGEN AUF GOTT: Vaterunser

German translation and publication of Dr. Errico's book *Setting a Trap for God.*

ES WERDE LICHT

German translation and publication of Dr. Errico's book *Let There Be Light: The Seven Keys.*

OTTO ACCORDI CON DIO: il Padre Nostro originario
Italian translation and publication of Dr. Errico's book *Setting a Trap for God.*

THE HOLY BIBLE FROM THE ANCIENT EASTERN TEXT

The entire Bible translated directly into English from Aramaic, the language of Jesus. There are approximately 12,000 major differences between this English translation and the many traditional versions of the Bible. One example: "For I the Lord thy God am a *jealous* God." (Exodus 20:5 King James Version) "For I the Lord your God am a *zealous* God." (Lamsa translation) Another example: "And *lead us* not into temptation . . ." (Matthew 6:13 KJV) "And *do not let us* enter into temptation . . . (Lamsa translation). $35.00

IDIOMS IN THE BIBLE EXPLAINED and A KEY TO THE ORIGINAL GOSPELS

Two books in one. In Book 1 (*Idioms in the Bible Explained*) Dr. Lamsa explains nearly 1000 crucial idioms and colloquialisms of Eastern speech that will enrich reading of the Old and New Testaments for student and general reader alike. Obscure and difficult biblical passages are listed and compared with the King James Version. These make clear the original meaning of such ancient idioms and assure that our grasp of the biblical message is more sound and rewarding. Example: "Lot's wife became a pillar of salt" means she suffered a stroke, became paralyzed and died.

Book 2 (*A Key to the Original Gospels*) explains how the gospels were written, the reason for two different genealogies, the conflicting stories of the birth of Jesus, and more. $14.95

THE KINGDOM ON EARTH

Part One—The Beatitudes, Part Two—The Lord's Prayer. Many scholars and teachers have dealt with the Sermon on the Mount, which has been called the "constitution of the Kingdom of heaven." None is more eminently qualified than Dr. Lamsa because no one else with his background has a similar knowledge of the Bible and of biblical times. With a warmth and understanding seldom equaled among contemporary scholars, Dr. Lamsa teaches the Beatitudes and the Lord's prayer in the light of Jesus' own language, people and times. $14.95

THE SHEPHERD OF ALL: The Twenty-Third Psalm

The Twenty-third Psalm, considered by many to be the most meaningful psalm in the Bible, is brought to life in a most vivid manner. Dr. Lamsa's ancestors for untold generations were sheep raising people and he was raised in a sheep camp. Based on his own personal experience as a shepherd, Dr. Lamsa interprets this beautiful and moving psalm in the light of Eastern biblical customs. $5.95

NEW TESTAMENT ORIGIN

Dr. Lamsa presents his theory for Aramaic as the original written language of the New Testament. To quote Dr. Lamsa in the forward of *New Testament Origin*: "The Aramaic text speaks for itself; it needs no defense. It is strongly supported by internal evidence, by the Aramaic style of writing, idioms, metaphors, and Oriental [Semitic] mannerisms of speech. Since Christianity is an Eastern religion, the Scriptures must have been written in an Eastern tongue. This fact will be recognized easily by any philologist familiar with Semitic languages. I am one of the millions in biblical lands—both Christians and Mohammedans—who believe that the New Testament was first written in Aramaic, and that our texts were carefully handed down from apostolic times." $5.95

AN HOUR WITH DR. GEORGE M. LAMSA (VIDEO)

Originally taped for TV in 1972 in Cadillac, Michigan under the title Lamsa at His Best. With the kind permission of Dr. Lamsa's family, we are now able to share this rare event in VHS format. A wonderful opportunity to see and hear Dr. Lamsa "live" as he answers many questions on the Bible from the Aramaic perspective. $29.95

Audio Tapes by Dr. Errico
(A sampling from classes, seminars and services)

BOOK OF THE REVELATION: An Esoteric-Aramaic Interpretation
This approach is not an exoteric-historical interpretation of the Revelation. It is an Aramaic metaphysical presentation that reveals various states of human consciousness. It shows how the living Christ in each individual triumphs over negative states of mind.

CROSS, ATONEMENT AND SACRED VIOLENCE
Is there a link between religion and violence? Does the Bible sanction violence? Dr. Errico presents a perceptive look at various biblical stories, the death of Jesus, the cross, and apocalyptic destruction.

DREAMS AND VISIONS
Dr. Errico delves into the significance of dreams and visions in Scripture as well as the various meanings to personal dream symbolism. He explores types of dream interpretation and teaches us how to interpret our own dreams.

THE GOSPEL OF JOHN
Based on his translation from the Aramaic text of John, Dr. Errico presents a profound and metaphysical study of John's view of Jesus.

JESUS' BIRTH AND GENEALOGY
The real meaning of the "Virgin Birth" story and the genealogy as told in the gospel of Matthew.

JESUS' HEALING METHODS
Jesus had no set healing method, but he used many different methods depending on the circumstances and the person seeking healing. A must for anyone who wants to understand the healing process.

KINGDOM OR THE CROSS
There are two messages stemming from the New Testament — *The Kingdom* and *The Cross*. Which of the two did Jesus proclaim? Was the cross necessary? Is the kingdom of heaven (God) present or do we

look to the future for its manifestation?

THE LORD'S PRAYER IN ARAMAIC
Learn to pronounce the Lord's Prayer (Mt. 6:9-13) in Aramaic, a word at a time, a line at a time.

MYSTERY OF THE RESURRECTION
What really happened on Easter morning? What influence did the death of Jesus have upon his apostles and disciples? Why did only those who believed in Jesus see him after the resurrection? A detailed study of the biblical resurrection and appearance episodes of Jesus.

MOSES: LIBERATOR / REVELATOR / TERMINATOR / MAGICIAN
Was Moses a real person? What does his name signify? What is the significance of the various names of God revealed to Moses? What are the spiritual and metaphysical meanings to this book. These are just a few of the questions Dr. Errico explores in this seminar.

NEW LIGHT ON CHRISTMAS / A CHRISTMAS CONSCIOUSNESS
Two intriguing messages that bring new understanding and insight to the meaning of Christmas.

SIGNS AND WONDERS IN MATTHEW
Topics include: *The Cursing of the Fig Tree, The Coin in the Mouth of the Fish, The Multiplication of the **Loaves and Fish.***

TREE OF GOOD AND EVIL
The Adam and Eve story has been interpreted as: 1) The fall of humankind; 2) The origin of sin; 3) The origin of evil; 4) The origin of death; 5) The origin of sex. In this talk Dr. Errico reveals what the story is really about.

TRANSCENDING HUMAN SUFFERING: STORY OF JOB
Is human suffering necessary? Why is the human family exposed to so much pain and injustice? Can we come to an understanding of and transcend our personal pain? These questions and more are explored.

NOTES

NOTES

NOTES

NOTES